AUDACITY OF JESUS

THE SON, THE LAMB, THE LION,
THE MESSIAH, AND
HIS
MISSION

OAKEY CHIKERE CHIKERERE

AUDACITY OF JESUS

Copyright ©2025 Oakey Chikere Chikerere
ISBN: 978-1-965593-68-4

All rights reserved. No part of this publication may be reproduced, distributed, or transmitted in any form or by any means, including photocopying, recording, or other electronic or mechanical methods without the prior written permission of the author except in the case of brief quotations embodied in reviews and certain other non-commercial uses permitted by copyright law.

Published by Cornerstone Publishing

A Division of Cornerstone Creativity Group LLC
Info@thecornerstonepublishers.com
www.thecornerstonepublishers.com

Author's Contact

To book the author to speak at your next event or to order bulk copies of this book, please, use the information below:

codlife5959@gmail.com

Printed in the United States of America.

DEDICATION

Dedicated to every believer who identified with Apostle Paul's resolve.

"...*what things were gain to me, those I counted loss for Christ...*

I count all things but loss for the Excellency of the knowledge of Christ Jesus my Lord: for whom I have suffered the loss of all things, and do count them but dung (rubbish), that I may win Christ."

— *Philippians 3:7-9*

Audacity of Jesus

..."Who do people say the son of man is?"

— Mt. 16:13b

CONTENTS

DEDICATION iii

SCRIPTURES vii

INTRODUCTION xiii

1. Birthplace, Geographical Location, Nativity And People. 1
2. The Genealogy Of Jesus Christ 37
3. The Wages Of Sin 155
4. The Life, Tradition, And Women In The Genealogy Of Jesus Christ 179
5. The Gospel 215

SCRIPTURES

DIVINE CONFESSION – CONFIRMATION

¹⁴ They replied, "Some say John the Baptist; others say Elijah; and still others, Jeremiah or one of the prophets."

¹⁵ "But what about you?" he asked. "Who do you say I am?"

¹⁶ Simon Peter answered, "You are the Messiah, the Son of the living God."

— *Matthew 16:14-16 (NIV)*

PROPHETIC REVELATION CONFIRMATION

Who has believed our message and to whom has the arm of the Lord been revealed?

² He grew up before him like a tender shoot, and like a root out of dry ground. He had no beauty or majesty to attract us to him, nothing in his appearance that we should desire him.

³ He was despised and rejected by mankind, a man of suffering, and familiar with pain. Like one from whom people hide their faces he was despised, and we held him in low esteem.

4 *Surely he took up our pain and bore our suffering,*

yet we considered him punished by God, stricken by him, and afflicted.

5 *But he was pierced for our transgressions, he was crushed for our iniquities; the punishment that brought us peace was on him, and by his wounds we are healed.*

6 *We all, like sheep, have gone astray, each of us has turned to our own way; and the Lord has laid on him the iniquity of us all.*

7 *He was oppressed and afflicted, yet he did not open his mouth; he was led like a lamb to the slaughter, and as a sheep before its shearers is silent, so he did not open his mouth.*

8 *By oppression and judgment he was taken away. Yet who of his generation protested? For he was cut off from the land of the living; for the transgression of my people he was punished.*

9 *He was assigned a grave with the wicked, and with the rich in his death, though he had done no violence, nor was any deceit in his mouth.*

10 *Yet it was the Lord's will to crush him and cause him to suffer, and though the Lord makes his life an offering for sin, he will see his offspring and prolong his days, and the will of the Lord will prosper in his hand.*

¹¹ After he has suffered, he will see the light of life and be satisfied; by his knowledge my righteous servant will justify many, and he will bear their iniquities.

¹² Therefore I will give him a portion among the great, and he will divide the spoils with the strong, because he poured out his life unto death, and was numbered with the transgressors. For he bore the sin of many, and made intercession for the transgressors.

— **Isaiah 53:1-12**

DIVINE PROPHECY AND THE LIGHT CONFIRMATION

Nevertheless, there will be no more gloom for those who were in distress. In the past he humbled the land of Zebulun and the land of Naphtali, but in the future he will honor Galilee of the nations, by the Way of the Sea, beyond the Jordan.

² The people walking in darkness have seen a great light; on those living in the land of deep darkness a light has dawned.

³ You have enlarged the nation and increased their joy; they rejoice before you as people rejoice at the harvest, as warriors rejoice when dividing the plunder.

⁴ For as in the day of Midian's defeat, you have shattered the yoke that burdens them, the bar across their shoulders, the rod of their oppressor.

⁵ *Every warrior's boot used in battle and every garment rolled in blood will be destined for burning, will be fuel for the fire.*

*— **Isaiah 9:1-5***

⁶ *For to us a child is born, to us a son is given, and the government will be on his shoulders. And he will be called.*

Wonderful Counselor, Mighty God, Everlasting Father, Prince of Peace.

⁷ *Of the greatness of his government and peace there will be no end. He will reign on David's throne and over his kingdom, establishing and upholding it with justice and righteousness from that time on and forever. The zeal of the Lord Almighty will accomplish this.*

*— **Isaiah 9:6-7(NIV)***

GOD'S WORD OF LIFE – CONFIRMATION

"1 In the beginning was the Word, and the Word was with God, and the Word was God. 2 He was with God in the beginning. 3 Through him, all things were made; without him, nothing was made that has been made. 4 In him was life, and that life was the light of all mankind. 5 The light shines in the darkness, and the darkness has not overcome it. **John 1:1-5 (NIV)**

SON OF GOD – CONFIRMATION

"⁴⁶ Nazareth! Can anything good come from there?" Nathanael asked. "Come and see," said Philip.

⁴⁷ When Jesus saw Nathanael approaching, he said of him, "Here truly is an Israelite in whom there is no deceit."

⁴⁸ "How do you know me?" Nathanael asked. Jesus answered, "I saw you while you were still under the fig tree before Philip called you."

⁴⁹ Then Nathanael declared, "Rabbi, you are the Son of God; you are the king of Israel."

—John 1:46-49

LAMB OF GOD – CONFIRMATION

John Testifies About Jesus

"The next day, John saw Jesus coming toward him and said, "Look, the Lamb of God, who takes away the sin of the world!"

—John 1:29

INTRODUCTION

A JOURNEY OF DIVINE WISDOM TO "CHANGE – SALVATION" FOR ABUNDANT LIFE AND ETERNAL KINGDOM

"You can't have a poem without a poet or a house without a house builder. You can't have design without an intelligent Designer….

On a microscopic level, we see that a single cell has ion-gated channels, voltage-gated channels, and members are potential. It was specifically designed to do one thing, i.e., carry a nerve impulse from one cell to another. When you look deep inside the cell, you find the DNA—the biological code of life that allows the cell to perpetuate itself. Within the cell, you have an incredibly complex biochemical code, and yet we are expected to believe that it "just happened by chance. Over and again, as you look throughout nature, you see what is almost like "neon arrow" pointing to a creator, an Intelligent Designer. That designer is God."

Brad Harrub, Phd. **Neurobiologist**

The Journey of "Change – Salvation" through divine wisdom for "Abundant Life" could only be attainable from a greater power, a greater force, and a greater Deity. This is the intelligent Creator God Almighty. The challenges and debates on "Change – Salvation" have mesmerized the intelligent community and have resulted in conflicts in corporate performances with life and death, family disorientation dramas, individual arrogance complacency, and dramatization of political leaders abuse of their offices. Even the theologians and the religious communities are worst off in their battle for "Change – Salvation" with the rest of the world.

Will God continue to grant His children in the world longevity, abundant life, and eternal Kingdom without "Change – Salvation" and redemption? OR will the fallen world continue to strife in rebellion, curses, and deception impressed on every generation of the world as a result of the sin of Adam and Eve?

> *[23] So the Lord God banished him (Adam) from the Garden of Eden to work the ground from which he had been taken. [25] After he drove the man out, he placed on the East side of the Garden of Eden cherubim and a flaming sword flashing back and forth to guard the way to the Tree of Life."*
>
> **— *Genesis 3:23-24 (NIV)***

God's plan for man in His creation was a perfect paradise, but God's enemy, Satan, doubled down on God's caretakers, beloved Adam and Eve, who listened to the voice and destructive plan of a fallen angel—Satan (Lucifer).

Successful studying and understanding the work of God and His creation call for critical attention and wisdom, not only human wisdom but divine wisdom. The story of Jesus Christ, His Ministry, and His Mission will unleash A Journey of Divine Wisdom to "Change – Salvation" for abundant life, which is a prelude (gateway) to external life and redemption.

Jesus Christ is a "Change – Salvation" agent appointed by the Intelligent Designer, Master Planner, the Omnipotent, Omnipresent, and Omniscience God to rescue, redeem, and obliterate the hazardous infectious sin epidemic tsunami that Satan and his co-hosts immersed on humanity through Adam and Eve.

This study of the "King of Kings, I am that I am, Rock of Ages," to name a few of His names, will try to define the Foundation, Structure, Character, and manifesto of the Kingdom of God, which the supreme intelligent creator built.

This comprehensive study will equally invoke the history and spectacle of God-elect—Abram, his descendants (Israel), the promised land, covenants, Jesus Christ the Redeemer, the Kingdom of God, and the Judgment of the world.

These form the focus of this Book:

"AUDACITY OF JESUS: THE SON, THE LAMB, THE LION, THE MESSIAH, AND HIS MISSION."

However, God's master plan is engrafted in His will, which governs all things created on Earth. God moves on His plans by exploring His Word, His chosen prophets, angels, Son, and Spirit, including places and times. God equally established Covenants, Rules, Commandments, and degrees to guide and control His creation.

The Bible scriptures captured the works of God as they were established and perfected according to His will, as it is written by Moses:

> *"He is the Rock, his works are perfect, and all his ways are just. A faithful God who does no wrong, upright and just is he."*

— *Deut. 32:4 (NIV)*

Many have written materials on the authenticity and truth of God's Word and His creativity, but still, there is a need and shortage of more apologetic materials to present the defense and the truth about the love and perfect work of God.

The Almighty God is not a respecter of persons, and He cannot lie. He is the Lord of yesterday, today, and tomorrow. He is not a person that He could lie… neither is He a man that can change. Even God Himself bears witness to His sovereignty.

"God saw all that he had made, and it was very good. And there was evening, and there was morning—the sixth day."

— *Genesis 1:31(NIV)*

God loves His creations and cannot abandon man, irrespective of our sinful nature. He is a compassionate Father. About 300 years ago, God, in His infinite mercy and love, enacted a covenant with His faithful son that He found worthy of His trust, Abram, to start the process of a divine master plan to reclaim and redeem His creation in the fallen world.

[1] The Lord had said to Abram, "Go from your country, your people, and your father's household to the land I will show you.

[2] "I will make you into a great nation, and I will bless you; I will make your name great, and you will be a blessing.

[3] I will bless those who bless you, and whoever curses you I will curse; and all peoples on earth will be blessed through you."

— *Genesis 12:1-3*

The call of Abram and the history of his descendants is a sensory gateway to this spiritual journey:

"Audacity of Jesus: The Son, The Lamb, The Lion, The Messiah, and his mission."

The fall of man grieved God's Heart because Adam jeopardized God's wisdom, which He employed in the creation of the world. However, God Himself acknowledged the beauty and splendor of His handwork and blessed it.

> *"God blessed them and said to them, 'Be fruitful and increase in number; fill the earth and subdue it. Rule over the fish in the sea and the birds in the sky and over every living creature that moves on the ground.'"*

— *Genesis 1:28*

The failure of Adam was doom for all mankind. The Almighty God banished Adam and Eve, as we see it in Genesis 3:23-24. God rejected man and drove him out of the Garden of Eden, which was bestowed with the Tree of Life. And the LORD GOD said:

> *"The man has now become like one of us, knowing good and evil. He must not be allowed to reach out his hand and take also from the tree of life and eat and live forever."*

— *Genesis 3:22*

In the last 200 years, many books and studies have been published about Jesus Christ of Nazareth. And yet more books are being written today in the search of the truth about Jesus. The critics generate ad-hoc questions and furnish mystical answers to support and justify their skepticism (doubt).

The only way to reach a meritorious conclusion will be the availability of more books so the readers will have the opportunity to expunge the truth. As Milo Connick wrote:

> *"Unfortunately, the personal and professional demands made of most readers do not permit them the luxury of acquiring a complete sampling of the tempting variety of books provided by publishers. The readers are compelled the purchase only a few offerings; thus, they run the risk of an unbalanced diet."*

The reason for this book, *Audacity of Jesus: The Son, Lamb, The Lion, The Messiah, and His Mission*, is to push the agenda about the truth, the light, the promise, the covenant, the life, the ministry and the mission of Jesus Christ of Nazareth. The millennial will find this book so interesting and entertaining to read, while it might equally hold some 21st-century critics of the Christian religion and the subject of Jesus Christ, His Father God, breathless.

My intent in this study is to combine oral, verbal and historic Greeks that presents a breath-taking narrative sensitize the life and death of Jesus Christ.

Connick, Jesus: The Man, The Mission and the Message. (Prentice-Hall, Inc., Englewood Cliffs,) N.J 1963. Which I have been opportune to assimilate. However, the last 18 years since I became a "Born-Again Believer" have been very phenomenal on my journey for salvation, adding faith and grace virtue to my ministry and mission.

The search, research for materials, and trials have empowered my zeal and spirit to different exposures concerning literal styles and written forms, thus indulging in some unpopular, literally grotesque (awkwardness). Hence, I humbly take a bow and ask my readers and critics to spear the chipmunk dancing among the street squirrels.

My Goal in this study is that it will be prospective and inspiring to evoke new enthusiasm among millennials who seek to reach the meritorious conclusion "That Jesus Christ is the Son of God, the Lion of Judah, and the Messiah of the world, and His mission is to redeem the perishing world."

In order to help me reach this milestone, I urge you and pray that you will enjoy spending time reading this for your best friend (because friends do not allow friends to drive drunk) and spread the gospel of our LORD Jesus Christ by asking your family and friends to read this book, with a promise that will 'change' their life. This book will usher in a new awesome relationship spiritually with our Lord Jesus Christ and His passion.

The light of Jesus has driven out every darkness that confronted me, the author, and many other believers. So, I am a living witness.

Many years ago, I thought that diligently seeking and following (Born-again Christians), God was for the Noods and wasted people. Not realizing that I was the one dead and blinded spiritually. I was found. The year 1999 became a landmark of a new dawn in my life.

The truth and the fact is that I have struggled with careers, finances, marriage, business, sickness, and imprisonment, but the good news is that I am still standing. God's grace and love have manifested in every area of my life.

I am still standing as I surrender to divine providence.

Aliluyya, Aliyah… today, as the light of God shines upon me…

I claim my sonship as;

A DISCIPLE, A TEACHER, A PASTOR, A WRITER, AN INVENTOR, AND AN ARTIST…

It's my hope and desire that reading this book will bring light to your life that the darkness (enemy-satan) will not be able to put off or comprehend. I could sense and feel the anointing of the Holy Spirit engulfing your spirit. What you are experiencing right now, reading this book, will transform your life. Pray that God will complete what He has started in your life today. Amen.

In conclusion to the introduction to this book are two parallel scriptural notes that summarize the entire study.

The first is written by Feinbery…

"Thus, the Lord will make good His truth, His promise, made to Abraham, Isaac, and Jacob. (To Abraham, Gen. 12:2-3, to Isaac, 26:24; to Jacob, 28:13-14,) The return from captivity could only be a fair test of a greater

display of God's grace in the coming reign of the Messiah, the purpose of all God's dealings with Israel's promise to Abraham and his seed."

Finally, the second writer, Anders...

"Micah's book ends where Israel's story began with the promises to Abraham (Gen. 12). A thousand years separated Abraham and Micah, but God still remembered His promise and kept it. The present situation may look dim and dark, covered in divine judgment. But (2) Feinberg, the minor prophets, moody). But God listens when His people pray and comes to redeem them as He did in Egypt. Almost a thousand years after Micah, God came in person of His son, Jesus Christ, to prove once and for all that He is faithful to His covenant promises."

To drive this message home to all my beloved readers, let it press in your heart with all diligence that God's purpose for Israel and all generations will come to pass (fulfillment). We are witnessing most of the perils prophesied in the scripture. The earthquakes, all kinds of tribulations, and murder.

Anders Holman Old Testament commentary. War, family, violence, parents against children, hurricanes, church division, political unrest, all kinds of religion, and the explosion of knowledge. All these tribulations point to the end of time. "Jesus is coming soon." This is the time to prepare. Men should repent and ask God for forgiveness for eternal kingdom.

O. C Chikere

CHAPTER ONE

BIRTHPLACE, GEOGRAPHICAL LOCATION, NATIVITY AND PEOPLE

BIRTHPLACE OF JESUS CHRIST

He rules the world with truth and grace,

And makes the nations prove

The glories of His righteousness,

And wonders of His love,

And wonders of His love,

And wonders, wonders, of His love.

— A stanza from the song Joy to the World by Isaac Watts

The story of Jesus paints a spectacular Hollywood-Disney satire movie picture, set up as if predestined for an Oscar-winning classic. Such historic awards come with iconic locations and showcases at grand theaters.

However, the similarity between Jesus' story and Hollywood movies may lie in their generic differences—spectacle and characteristics, periods, lands, people, civilizations, culture, tradition, politics, religion, and geographical locations. These differences shape and define the history that influences their way of life.

In the case of Jesus' story, the origins can be traced back to the creation of the world: "The Garden of Eden and Adam and Eve." Apostle John, a disciple of Jesus Christ and a key witness from Jesus' adult life up until his death, wrote in one of his epistles:

> *"In the beginning was the Word, and the Word was with God, and the Word was God. The same was in the beginning with God. All things were made by Him, and without Him was not anything made that was made. In Him was life, and the life was the light of men. And the light shineth in darkness; and darkness comprehended it not."*

—*John 1:1-5 (KJV)*

Apostle John provides clear proof that Jesus Christ is the "Son of God." His writings about the birth of Jesus show that He existed before the creation of the world. Jesus is a spiritual being from the eternal kingdom. You may ask, what did John mean by this statement? This study will address and answer such questions in future chapters of this book.

However, Connick wrote an interesting piece concerning the "birthplace" of Jesus Christ:

> *"Jesus was a Jew. His people adhered to diverse theologies, embraced differing cultures, and (to some degree) exhibited varying racial characteristics. One of their most distinctive features was their sense of history. It bound them together and made them a separate people. When they celebrated the Passover, read in the Synagogues, and taught their children the tradition of the elders, they nourished their feelings of uniqueness... In Western civilization, a man's life begins at birth. For a Chinese person, it commences at conception. But for a Jew, life starts with Abraham, the traditional ancestor of his people. This is why Matthew began his account of Jesus with the words, 'Abraham was the father of Isaac.'"*

— *Mathew 1:2*

The journey and drama in this book begin with Abram since we have established that Jesus is a Jew. God is the producer and master architect of His creativity, which has placed everything in the world that was not there in the beginning.

Is that not super wonderful? (God's divine master plan). As God was diligently drafting the plan of His creativity, He mirrored Himself in the deity of His beloved Son, Jesus, on whom His Holy Spirit descended as a dove at Jordan, with a loud voice:

"This is my beloved Son, in whom I am well pleased."

— *Matthew 3:17*

Perchance, man eloped and became elusive. Lo and behold, man chickened out and embarrassingly took up the task of generativity—to originate and produce—as John Kotre wrote:

"To invest one's substance in forms of life and work that will outlive the self."

— *J. Kotre, Outliving the Self (Baltimore: John Hopkins University Press, 1984), P.10.*

With the fall of man, his prerogative changed, and God allowed man to have the mind to choose between life and death.

In furtherance of God's creativity, the Lord said to Abraham:

"Leave your country, your people, and your father's household, and go to the land I will show you."

— *Genesis 12:1 (NIV)*

This command, as much as it sounds like a movie, was clear and persuasive, especially in understanding what took place many years ago—in the medieval period around 538 BC—when there were no scientific compasses or GPS. There was no formal or institutional form of worship at the time, either. What needs to be established here is that there was no form of worship, so one cannot contrast that Abraham had a prior relationship with God before his "calling."

Like the concept of human validation, Abram did not seek a second opinion. Neither did he search for a prophet to determine his future and faith, nor did he ask for a sign to confirm whether God was the originator of such an instruction to migrate to an unknown destination.

What would be your reaction to such a call to depart from your family without notice? Would you obey without hesitation or "fake it till you believe it"? Your answer is as good as any other. But Abram, as we read, obeyed, packed his possessions, and departed Hebron. This single act of trust earned him an Oscar Award—"Father of Faith." To some Christians, this divine call sounds and appears delusional and hard to absorb.

Abram, as we are told, was not a troubled young star. In fact, he was seventy-five years old when he departed from his family and homeland, meaning that Abram had baggage and responsibilities.

Moses' response to the call of Abram is recorded:

"So Abram left, as the Lord had told him, and Lot went with him. Abram was seventy-five years old when he set out from Haran. He took his wife Sarai, his nephew

> *Lot, all the possessions they had accumulated, and the people they had acquired in Haran, and they set out for the land of Canaan, and they arrived there."*

— *Genesis 12:1-5 (NIV)*

Let's examine ourselves and be honest with our answers. How would you respond to an unknown caller today, pretending to be God, asking you to abandon your family and country for an unknown destination? Do you honestly believe you would obey without struggle?

Most of us, even with the lessons learned from this story, would still fail the test of God's calling. Many Christians have missed divine opportunities by not obeying the voice of God due to their lack of faith and obedience.

Let me draw your attention to the introduction of this book: *A Journey of Divine Wisdom to 'Change' for Abundant Life*. Be patient and stay focused with me. The calling of Abram and his departure is a lesson on "change – salvation" in life. You can be successful in your life and everyday assignments by adopting the spirit of "change – salvation" in respect and obedience to your emotions and trials.

Obedience will deliver you from every court of pride and humility when you adopt an attitude of change.

> *"Long ago, Plato understood that a wise 'charioteer' was needed to balance the pull of his two horses, 'Desire' and 'Obedience.' Too often over the next two thousand*

years, however, the more people thought about it, the more important the paradigm of intellect over emotion and obedience over desire became. This culminated in Marxist and Skinnerian belief in utter obedience and rationality to the exclusion of emotion. But Plato's view is proven right by long-time follow-up. We ignore desire and emotion at our peril. The sweet rational enlightenment of the French Revolution worked for about a year; then, all hell broke loose. By ignoring the 'desire' of greedy capitalism for decades, disciplined Marxism, too, has failed."

— George E. Vaillant, MD, Aging Well (Little, Brown and Company, New York; NY, 2002) P.60.

There is a need to change, to balance obedience and desire. One may ask, how? The freedom found and preached from the "message of the cross," which is the foundation of this study, "Audacity of Jesus," will continue to deliver man from obscurity and darkness into light.

An American slang says, "Talk is cheap," but to "walk the walk" is a different ball game. We must follow through on what we preach and profess. Change is possible as we emulate the lifestyle of Jesus.

The freedom of abundant life and the eternal Kingdom is imminent. While excuses have robbed many God-called champions of their destiny opportunities, if they recover from their slumber, they must embrace obedience through wisdom.

They must recognize that trust, obedience, humility, and faithfulness are the wheels on which divine calling and every assignment thrive.

This study must prospectively embrace oral narrative, historical, and theological reviews so that readers can, to some extent, relate to and identify with the country (village) life of Jesus Christ. Jesus was born a Semite since His ancestor Abraham was a Semite Jew. Let me draw your attention to an objective conclusion written by Goethe:

"Whoever the poet will understand must go into the poet's land."

People are generally, to some degree, reflections of their places of origin and nativity, especially when they are born and raised in the same community. Jewish-Hebrew communities instill a sense of integrity that demands respect, peace, unity, and emotional bonds with sound communal fellowship. Similarly, Jesus' upbringing is reflective of His native identity. Judaism was a common religion during the birth of Jesus, and the synagogue was a ritual place for socialization and worship.

Jesus' identity as a Jew can be compared equally to some Western cultures, as Connick wrote:

"Someone remarked that the British and the Americans are united by a common culture and common custom and divided by a common language. There is much truth in this statement; however, language is but one of the distinct

characteristics of a country's people. Such characteristics as clothes, mannerisms, and attitude also enable one to recognize a stranger in a foreign land. So important a role is played by one's native land in the life of any person, that in order to understand Jesus, we must first become familiar with His homeland."

— Connick C. Milo

We can recognize Connick's optimism in characteristics that define people's lives and history (nativity). Goethe's observation is absolutely true and connects with Connick's views. Both writers converge at the focal point that Jesus' homeland is the foundation of the model of "Jesus' House," and God is the architectural engineer.

HOMELAND

"I will give this land to your family forever."

— Genesis 12:7b (CEV)

Jesus' homeland is designated with many names ("Canaan," "Promised Land"). The "Promised Land" comes from God's promise to Abram (Genesis 12). Today, the land of Canaan and Jerusalem is known as the "Holy Land." Thus, the narrative of Moses about Jesus' ancestors and God's promise to Abram:

"Terah decided to move from Ur to the land of Canaan. He took along Abram, Sarai, and his grandson Lot, the

> *son of Haran, but when they came to the city of Haran, they decided to settle there instead. Terah lived to be two hundred five years old and died in Haran."*

— *Genesis 11:31 (NIV)*

> *"...It came to pass that when the sun went down, and it was dark, behold, a smoking furnace and a burning lamp that passed between those pieces. On that same day, the Lord made a covenant with Abram, saying, 'Unto thy seed, I will give this land, from the river of Egypt unto the great river, the river Euphrates: The Kenites, and the Kenizzites, and the Hittites, and the Kadmonites, and the Perizzites, and the Raphaim, and the Amorites and the Canaanites, and the Girgashites, and the Jebusites.'"*

— *Genesis 15:17-21 (KJV)*

We are able to understand and establish the homeland of Jesus Christ, the geographical location, and His people, dating back to the 12th to 11th centuries BC. God Almighty blessed the Children of Israel, who were coming out of the land of Egypt as slaves, with vast lands running from the Nile River up to the Tigris-Euphrates River. With increased population and successful wars and battles, they acquired land across Syria and Palestine. In fact, civilization flourished, and Palestine soon became a hotspot like Egypt and Assyria-Babylonia.

Palestine developed in commerce and became a link and center for Africa, Europe, and Asia. However, the influx of migration and development created endless battles and confrontations for land ownership and boundary procurements between Israel and its neighboring countries. In response to these conflicts, Connick, in his review, wrote:

> "Today, it is a pawn in the power struggle between East and West. It is little wonder since nearby are over half of the world's proven oil supplies. In Jesus' days, the boundaries of Palestine were as elastic as a rubber band. They expanded in periods of national weakness. A favorite biblical phrase defined the populated limits of the country as extending from Dan (nestled in the foothills of Mt. Hermon in the North) to Beersheba, a desert outpost in the South. The country was bordered on the north by Phoenicia (modern Lebanon), Syria on the east by the Arabian desert, on the south by the Arabian desert and the Sinai peninsula, and on the west by the Mediterranean Sea. Its length was about 150 miles, and its width varied from 35 miles in the north to 70 miles in the south. It contained only 10,000 square miles, making it roughly equivalent to New Hampshire or Vermont, one-fifth the size of Pennsylvania or England, and one-fifteenth the size of California. A jet plane can fly across its widest part in a matter of minutes."

SOME IMPORTANT PLACES OF INTEREST

- The plain of Sharon / Mt. Carmel
- The city of Caesarea
- The red sandy soil of Sharon
- Five towns of Philistine: Gaza, Ashkelon, Ashdod, Ekron, and Gath
- The western highlands: Mountain ranges in Syria and Lebanon
- The highlands of Galilee
- The plains of Esdraelon and Jezreel
- The city of Jerusalem
- The city of Babylon
- The country of Judah
- The city of Samaria
- The city of Nazareth
- The city of Bethlehem

MAP OF ISRAEL

OME IMPORTANT PLACES OF INTEREST

As the study seeks to paint and bring to the minds of the readers every detail possible to place Jesus Christ in His homeland, we will equally examine and evaluate His life experiences using the facts available. The study will advance to explore Jesus Christ as the epitome of Christianity and the Kingdom of God. These landmarks draw significant attention worldwide, especially among Christian enthusiasts in the 21st century.

The intent is to create awareness and inject a new sense of optimism for those hoping to visit and explore the magnificent tourist attractions of the historic Holy Land. The Holy Land is endowed with numerous picturesque landscapes. However, for the sake of perspective, the list is reduced to twelve of the most important sites that the author believes might spark some excitement and, at the same time, reinforce the authenticity of the story of Jesus Christ of Nazareth.

THE RIVER OF KISHON SISERA

"From the heavens, the stars fought; from their courses, they fought against Sisera. The river Kishon swept them away; the age-old river, the river Kishon. March on, my soul; be strong!"

— Judges 5:20-21 (NIV)

This River Kishon Sisera is a memorable and miraculous site in the history of Israel. The story in Judges 5 relates the song of Deborah and Barak, son of Abinoam, which says:

"When the princes in Israel take the lead, when the people willingly offer themselves—praise the Lord! Hear this, you kings! Listen, you rulers!

I will sing to the Lord, I will sing; I will make music to the Lord, the God of Israel."

— Judges 5:2-3 (NIV)

According to the story in Judges 5, Deborah and Barak fought Sisera's (Canaanite) army at Megiddo. As the prophetic word of John in Revelation 16:16 foretells the Battle of Armageddon, depicted as the "Hills of Megiddo," Deborah and Barak miraculously crushed Sisera's army. The gates of Heaven opened, and a rainstorm poured on the Kishon River, causing it to overflow. The Canaanite army, which outnumbered the army of Deborah and Barak, became trapped in the muddy clay, unable to escape. It was a divine intervention—a miraculous deliverance for Israel.

THE PLAIN OF SHARON

The plain of Sharon, with Mount Carmel at its base, extends to the historic harbor of Jaffa. This port was well-known, and several historic activities were recorded at this location in the Bible.

> *"Hiram, king of Tyre, shipped the cedars of Lebanon, which King Solomon used to build the great temple in Jerusalem."*
>
> *— 2 Chronicles 2:15 (NIV)*

Legend has it that all shipwrecked gold, silver, and precious stones from the seas flowed to Jaffa. Additionally, the famous prophet Jonah, who tried to escape from answering God's call, fled to the Jaffa seaport to board a ship headed to Tarshish.

> *"But Jonah ran away from the Lord and headed for Tarshish. He went down to Jaffa, where he found a ship bound for that port. After paying the fare, he went aboard and sailed for Tarshish to flee from the Lord."*

— *Jonah 1:3 (NIV)*

Another remarkable event took place in Jaffa: Simon, a tanner, housed his guest, Simon Peter, who went to pray on the roof of his house. Peter had a vision while praying that led to the evangelism of the Romans:

> *"He fell into a trance. He saw heaven open and something like a large sheet being let down to earth by its four corners. It contained all kinds of four-footed animals, as well as reptiles of the earth and birds of the air. Then a voice told him, 'Get up, Peter, kill and eat.'*
>
> *'Surely not, Lord!' Peter replied. 'I have never eaten anything impure or unclean.'*
>
> *The voice spoke to him a second time, 'Do not call anything impure that God has made clean.' This happened three times, and immediately, the sheet was taken back to heaven."*

— *Acts 10:11-16 (NIV)*

THE CITY OF CAESAREA

Around 22 BC, King Herod the Great built a new city and named it Caesarea in honor of Augustus Caesar. The city grew to become the most important in Sharon during the historic days, serving as the main seaport and capital of Palestine. Caesarea became a popular landmark in ancient history for over five hundred years. The biblical account documents Apostle Paul's imprisonment for two years while awaiting trial before the court:

> *"Then King Agrippa said to Paul, 'You have permission to speak for yourself.' So Paul motioned with his hand and began his defense: 'King Agrippa, I consider myself fortunate to stand before you today as I make my defense against all the accusations of the Jews.'"*
>
> *— Acts 26:1-2 (NIV)*

Equally, the Bishop of Caesarea published a great book. As Connick notes, in the fourth century, Eusebius, Bishop of Caesarea, wrote his monumental history. The soil of Sharon, with its red sand, is very fertile. The farmers produced large quantities of oranges and citrus fruits, boosting agricultural production for the European market. Even the lilies of the valley of the Plain of Sharon are very beautiful during springtime. In fact, Jesus mentioned the wildflowers and roses of Sharon in His teachings:

> *"And why do you worry about clothes? See how the lilies of the field grow. They do not labor or spin. Yet I tell you that not even Solomon in all his splendor was dressed like one of these."*
>
> — ***Matthew 6:28-29 (NIV)***

THE FIVE CITIES OF PHILISTINE: GAZA, ASHKELON, ASHDOD, EKRON, AND GATH

These five cities define the land of Philistine, with the city of Gaza as the most popular. Gaza has been nicknamed "Gaza Strip," which has become home to over one million refugees and immigrants. The city of Gaza is also a trans-trade route between Egypt, Africa, and the Northern countries. These five cities formed a confederation in order to war against Israel. The "Gaza Strip" (city of Gaza) has become the battleground of modern conflicts between Israel and Palestine. Another historic event that took place on this plain was the battle that cost the lives of King Saul and his sons.

> *"Now the Philistines fought against Israel; the Israelites fled before them, and many fell slain on Mount Gilboa. The Philistines pressed hard after Saul and his sons, and they killed his sons, Jonathan, Abinadab, and Malki-Shua. Saul said to his armor-bearer, 'Draw your sword and run me through, or these uncircumcised fellows will*

come and run me through and abuse me.' But his armor-bearer would not do it, so Saul took his own sword and fell on it."

— *1 Samuel 31:1-4 (NIV)*

The western highlands are another section of the Philistine that form the stronghold of the Holy Land. It has many hunting ranges in the southern mountain areas. The Syrian mountains are known for the production of cedar and lumber. In fact, history records that King Solomon acquired all the cedar logs he used to build the temple from Mount Hermon. The Arabs call it "Sheikh Mountain" because it is the chief of them all. This mountain is also recorded in the Bible as the place where Jesus was transfigured in the presence of His disciples:

"And after six days, Jesus took Peter, James, and John with Him and led them up a high mountain, where they were all alone. There, He was transfigured before them. His clothes became dazzling white, whiter than anyone in the world could bleach them. And there appeared before them Elijah and Moses, who were talking with Jesus."

— *Mark 9:2-4 (NIV)*

South of Galilee, the Esdraelon, and Jezreel plains stretch across the northwestern side of the Mediterranean. The Kishon River divides the Esdraelon plain into halves, creating the valley of Jezreel. These plains are described as follows:

> "The two plains were famous as the most traveled pass across the country. From Egypt to Damascus, the route followed the seacoast from Gaza to Carmel, through Esdraelon and Jezreel, and then across the Jordan Valley. To protect the trade route and defend it from marauding Bedouins, a mighty fortress was constructed at Beth-Shean at the eastern end of Jezreel. The region was so renowned for its fertility that the sages of Israel sang, 'If the Garden of Eden is in the land of Israel—then its gate is at Beth-Shean.'"

Another important historical location is Mount Carmel, which is part of the plains of Esdraelon. On the northwestern side, a miraculous defeat of the 450 prophets of Baal took place, led by Prophet Elijah. These prophets were followers of King Ahab's wife, Jezebel, who worshiped Baal.

> "And Elijah replied, 'I have not troubled Israel, but you and your father's house have, in that you have forsaken the commandments of the LORD and followed Baal. Now, summon the people from all over Israel to meet me on Mount Carmel. And bring the 450 prophets of Baal and the 400 prophets of Asherah, who eat at Jezebel's table.' So Ahab sent word throughout all Israel and assembled the prophets on Mount Carmel."

— 1 Kings 18:18-20 (NIV)

> "Then Elijah said to them, 'I am the only one of the LORD's prophets left, but Baal has 450 prophets. Get two bulls for us. Let Baal's prophets choose one for themselves, and let them cut it into pieces and put it on the

wood, but not set fire to it. I will prepare the other bull and put it on the wood, but not set fire to it. Then you call on the name of your god, and I will call on the name of the LORD. The god who answers by fire—he is God.' Then all the people said, 'What you say is good.'"

"Elijah said to the prophets of Baal, 'Choose one of the bulls and prepare it first since there are so many of you. Call on the name of your god, but do not light the fire.' So they took the bull given to them and prepared it. Then they called on the name of Baal from morning till noon. 'O Baal, answer us!' they shouted. But there was no response; no one answered. And they danced around the altar they had made."

— *1 Kings 18:22-26 (NIV)*

"At noon, Elijah began to taunt them. 'Shout louder!' he said. 'Surely he is a god! Perhaps he is deep in thought, or busy, or traveling. Maybe he is sleeping and must be awakened.' So they shouted louder and slashed themselves with swords and spears, as was their custom until their blood flowed."

— *1 Kings 18:27-28 (NIV)*

"Then Elijah said to all the people, 'Come here to me.' They came to him, and he repaired the altar of the LORD, which had been torn down. Elijah took twelve stones, one for each of the tribes descended from Jacob, to whom the word of the LORD had come, saying, 'Your name shall be Israel.' With the stones, he built an altar

in the name of the LORD, and he dug a trench around it large enough to hold two seahs of seed. He arranged the wood, cut the bull into pieces, and laid it on the wood. Then he said to them, 'Fill four large jars with water and pour it on the offering and on the wood.' 'Do it again,' he said, and they did it again. 'Do it a third time,' he ordered, and they did it the third time. The water ran down around the altar and even filled the trench."

"At the time of sacrifice, the prophet Elijah stepped forward and prayed: 'LORD, the God of Abraham, Isaac, and Israel, let it be known today that you are God in Israel and that I am your servant and have done all these things at your command. Answer me, LORD, answer me, so these people will know that you, LORD, are God and that you are turning their hearts back again.' Then the fire of the LORD fell and burned up the sacrifice, the wood, the stones, and the soil, and also licked up the water in the trench. When all the people saw this, they fell prostrate and cried, 'The LORD—he is God! The LORD—he is God!'"

"Then Elijah commanded them, 'Seize the prophets of Baal. Don't let anyone get away!' They seized them, and Elijah had them brought down to the Kishon Valley and slaughtered there."

— *1 Kings 18:30-40 (NIV)*

Another miraculous event took place on Mount Carmel that shook the world in Israel. The same Prophet Elijah had predicted to King Ahab that there would be no rain for three years, and the land of Israel experienced drought and famine as a result.

After the killing of Baal's prophets at Mount Carmel, Elijah told King Ahab, who was weary and amazed, to go and eat and drink, for good news was coming—a sound of abundant rain.

> *"Then Elijah said to King Ahab, 'Go get something to eat and drink, for I hear a mighty rainstorm coming.' So Ahab went to eat and drink. But Elijah climbed to the top of Mount Carmel and bowed low to the ground and prayed with his face between his knees."*

> **— *1 Kings 18:41-42 (NLT)***

> *"Then he said to his servant, 'Go and look out toward the sea.' The servant went and looked, then returned to Elijah and said, 'I didn't see anything.' Seven times, Elijah told him to go and look. Finally, the seventh time, his servant told him, 'I saw a little cloud about the size of a man's hand rising from the sea.' Then Elijah shouted, 'Hurry to Ahab and tell him, "Climb into your chariot and go back home. If you don't hurry, the rain will stop you!"' And soon the sky was black with clouds. A heavy wind brought a terrific rainstorm, and Ahab left quickly for Jezreel."*

> **— *1 Kings 18:43-45 (NLT)***

THE CITY OF SAMARIA

The king, Omri, built up the city of Samaria into a great city. In fact, he made the city the capital of the Northern Kingdom. It is said that his son Ahab completed the construction of the city of Samaria. The city of Samaria equally played a very important part in the ministry of Jesus Christ. It was at "Jacob's well" at Nablus (Shechem) where Jesus had an encounter with a Samaritan woman. He requested water from the well, and Jesus promised her the water of life, "living water." This encounter led to the evangelism of the Samaritans, which brought backlash and criticism from His apostles because Samaritans were seen as outcasts. However, the good news was that around 128 BC, the Samaritans built their first temple on Mount Gerizim, which the Jewish leader John Hyrcanus destroyed 200 years after its completion.

> *"Sir," the woman said, "you must be a prophet. So tell me, why is it that you Jews insist that Jerusalem is the only place of worship, while the Samaritans claim that it is here at Mount Gerizim, where our ancestors worshiped?" Jesus replied, "Believe me, dear woman, the time is coming when it will no longer matter whether you worship the Father on this mountain or in Jerusalem."*
>
> *— John 4:19-21 (NIV)*

The city of Samaria is immersed in historic events. It was at about the "Ladder" when Jacob rested his head on a stone at night:

"As he slept, he dreamed of a stairway that reached from earth up to heaven. And he saw the angels of God going up and down the stairway. At the top of the stairway stood the LORD, and He said, 'I am the LORD, the God of your grandfather Abraham, and the ground you are lying on belongs to you. I am giving it to you and your descendants. Your descendants will be as numerous as the dust of the earth. They will spread out in all directions— to the west and the east, to the north and the south. And all the families of the earth will be blessed through you and your descendants.'"

— ***Genesis 28:12-14 (NIV)***

The priest of Shiloh, Eli, and the temple, along with his mentor, Prophet Samuel, add to the collective religious history that made Samaria an ancient historic enclave.

CITY OF JUDEA

Judea is a beautifully craggy plateau with its highest peak at 3,000 feet, displaying naturally dramatic scattered rocks. There is a mythical story behind its creation: an angel responsible for the proper distribution of rock and boulders flew over Palestine, but his mission came to a premature end when the bag broke over Judea. The mixture of these crest rocks, vegetation, olive orchards, and rich valleys creates plains for agricultural endowments. Bethany, the home of Biblical Mary, Martha, and Jesus' miraculous friend Lazarus (Luke), is also located here. The memorable valley of Eshcol, at the plain of Hebron, reinforces the story of Moses sending Joshua, Caleb, and a band of spies to explore the potential of the "Promised Land."

> *"When they reached the valley of Eshcol, they cut off a branch bearing a single cluster of grapes. Two of them carried it on a pole between them, along with some pomegranates and figs."*
>
> **— Numbers 13:23 (NIV)**

Furthermore, the story of Judea would seem incomplete without mention of some barren, bleak plains and Beersheba, which lies in the southernmost part of Palestine. This plain played a tremendous role in the lives of the patriarchs:

> *"It was there that Abraham planted a tamarisk tree and made a covenant with Abimelech."*
>
> **— Genesis 21:33 (NIV)**

> *"Then Abraham complained to Abimelech about a well of water that Abimelech's servants had seized. But Abimelech said, 'I don't know who has done this. You did not tell me, and I heard about it only today.' So Abraham brought sheep and cattle and gave them to Abimelech, and the two men made a treaty."*
>
> **— Genesis 21:25-27 (NIV)**

THE SEA OF GALILEE

The Sea of Galilee is a remarkable location in Israel. It receives the largest amount of water from the Jordan River. It is important to examine how Conder describes the course of the two rivers:

> *"...from Lake Huleh, the Jordan tumbles headlong down a narrow gorge in an almost continuous cascade. It drops nearly 700 feet in less than nine miles, and then, through a delta of its own deposits, it slides noisily into the Sea of Galilee. How appropriate that this river should be named Jordan, 'the Descender.'"*

The Sea of Galilee was very popular, with many dramatic events occurring there during the life and ministry of Jesus Christ. It has been called by several names: Chinnereth (Deuteronomy 3:17), Tiberias (John 6:1), and Gennesaret. In modern Israel, it is known as "Kinneret" because of the sea's shape—like a harp (Kinnor in Hebrew). The weather is sometimes extreme, bringing sudden storms, as written in the book of Mark:

> *"But soon, a fierce storm came up. High waves were breaking into the boat, and it began to fill with water. Jesus was sleeping at the back of the boat with His head on a cushion. The disciples woke Him up, shouting, 'Teacher, don't you care that we're going to drown?'*

> *When Jesus woke up, He rebuked the wind and said to the waves, 'Silence! Be still!' Suddenly, the wind stopped, and there was a great calm."*
>
> ### *— Mark 4:37-39 (NLT)*

The fishermen are conscious of these storms, so they make proper arrangements and provisions to secure their boats. Yet in winter, the sea draws many tourists to its banks. The Sea of Galilee bears witness to the early ministry of Jesus. Jesus healed many in Capernaum, and the city of Chorazin was criticized by Jesus for their lack of faith and belief in the good news:

> *"What sorrow awaits you, Chorazin and Bethsaida! For if the miracles I did in you had been done in Tyre and Sidon, their people would have repented of their sins long ago, clothing themselves in burlap and throwing ashes on their heads to show their remorse. I tell you, Tyre and Sidon will be better off on judgment day than you."*
>
> ### *— Matthew 11:21-22 (NLT)*

Jesus heard the news of John the Baptist's death and withdrew from entering Bethsaida (Luke 9:10). In Gadara, there is the story of Jesus casting out demons from a man, driving them into a herd of swine, which then plunged into the sea and drowned:

> *"'All right, go!' Jesus commanded them. So the demons came out of the men and entered the pigs, and the whole herd plunged down the steep hillside into the lake and*

drowned in the water. The herdsmen fled to the nearby town, telling everyone what had happened to the demon-possessed men. The entire town came out to meet Jesus, but they begged Him to go away and leave them alone."

— *Matthew 8:32-34 (NLT)*

No other place in Palestine witnessed more of Jesus' activities than the Sea of Galilee. It was here that He called His first disciples:

"One day, as Jesus was walking along the shore of the Sea of Galilee, He saw Simon and his brother Andrew throwing a net into the water, for they fished for a living. Jesus called out to them, 'Come, follow Me, and I will make you fishers of men.' And they left their nets at once and followed Him."

— *Mark 1:16-18 (NLT)*

The miracle of Peter casting his net for a "great" catch, the preaching from Peter's boat (Luke 5:1-11), and the witnessing to the multitude at Galilee could be described today as a "crusade at the Sea of Galilee":

"Jesus went out to the lake with His disciples, and a large crowd followed Him. They came from all over Galilee, Judea, Jerusalem, and Idumea, from east of the Jordan River, and even from as far north as Tyre and Sidon. The news about His miracles had spread far and wide, and vast numbers of people came to see Him."

— *Mark 3:7-8 (NLT)*

In summary, the Sea of Galilee could be described as "Jesus' amphitheater" for proclaiming the good news. The Sea of Galilee provided Jesus with security from the Sanhedrin court, a platform with fishermen's boats as a pulpit, a worship location away from city distractions, and a "Baptism" lagoon.

THE DEAD SEA

Finally, this historical inland sea, known as the "Dead Sea," will bring our exploration of Jesus' homeland to a close as we examine His nativity, people, mission, and life on earth.

The Dead Sea is located to the south of the Sea of Galilee, bordered by the highlands of Samaria and Galilee. It is estimated that the land is about three to fourteen miles wide and about 600 to 1,200 feet below sea level. The plain is a long valley that could expand to twice the size of Beersheba and Jericho.

The Arabs call it "The Ghor" or "Rift." Unlike other rivers in Israel, the Jordan River empties into the Dead Sea, bringing all its resources, but the Dead Sea does not let its waters flow out. The "Dead Sea" is a beneficiary, withholding all its benefits.

The length of the Dead Sea is approximately fifty miles, with a width of about ten miles. The Dead Sea has earned many names; one of them is the "Sea of Salt," as described by Moses in his writings:

> "All these were joined together in the valley of Siddim, which is the Salt Sea."

— Genesis 14:3 (KJV)

In the book of Deuteronomy, it is called the "Sea of Wilderness" (Deut 3:17), and Prophet Ezekiel referred to it as the "Eastern Sea":

> "And the eastside ye shall measure... and from the land of Israel by Jordan, from the border unto the 'east sea.' And this is the east side."

— Ezekiel 47:18 (KJV)

Some notable writers have also written about the Dead Sea. One of them, Zev Vilnay, wrote:

> "An average of six million tons of water pour into the Dead Sea daily, yet the level of the sea remains constant. The scorching sun and dry wind lap up the incoming waters almost as rapidly as they appear. The concentrated solutes remain, leaving the water oily to the touch and bitter to taste. When four buckets full are allowed to evaporate, one bucket full of salt and other minerals is left. The Dead Sea is an enormous storehouse of minerals: 22 billion tons of magnesium chloride, 1 billion tons of sodium chloride (salt), 7 million tons of calcium chloride, 2 million tons of potassium chloride, and 1 billion tons of magnesium bromide."

— Zev Vilnay, Israel Guide, 3rd ed. (Jerusalem: The Central Press, 1960), p.17.

The Dead Sea holds great potential for mineral wealth, but its waters are a challenge for water sports and recreation. The water is hazardous, and no marine life exists in the Dead Sea. In fact, many divers have lost their lives attempting to explore its waters. Connick wrote a parable about Palestine's two great seas:

> *"One is fresh, and fish are in it; splashes of green adorn its banks. Trees spread their branches over it and stretch out thirsty roots to sip its healing waters. Along its shores, children play, just as they did when He was there. He loved it. He could look across its silver surface as He spoke His parables. The Jordan River feeds this sea with sparkling water from the hills. Men build their homes near it, and birds nest there, and every kind of life is happier because it is there. The Jordan River flows south into another sea. Here, there is no splash of fish, no fluttering leaf, no song of birds, no children's laughter. Travelers choose another route unless on urgent business. The air hangs heavy above its waters, and neither man nor beast nor fowl will drink from it."*

These major rivers in Israel play very important roles, as they help define the characteristics of people around the world. Let's consider how Bruce Burton described the difference between the two seas of Palestine:

> *"It is not the Jordan that makes the difference; it empties the same good water into both seas. It is not the soil in which they lie nor the country roundabout. The difference is this: The Sea of Galilee receives but does not keep the*

Jordan. For every drop that flows into it, another drop flows out. The other sea (the Dead Sea) is shrewder, hoarding its incoming water jealously. It will not be tempted into any generous impulse. Every drop it gets, it keeps. The Sea of Galilee gives and lives. This other sea gives nothing. It is dead. There are two seas in Palestine, and there are two kinds of people in the world."

— Bruce Burton, "There Are Two Seas," Me Calls, LV, No. 7 (1927), p. 7 (Reprint).

The Dead Sea holds memorable history and stories that define its location and geographical significance. The destroyed cities of Sodom and Gomorrah once stood around the Dead Sea (Genesis 18:20-24). Jesus used the perils of these cities in His teachings. In Matthew's Gospel, Jesus said:

"Verily I say unto you, it shall be more tolerable for the land of Sodom and Gomorrah in the day of judgment than for the city, than for those who will not receive His disciples and their message."

— Matthew 18:15 (NIV)

THE CITY OF JERUSALEM

The city of Jerusalem is known as the Holy City. It is the epicenter—the political Washington—of Israel, the seat of all spiritual activities that include Judaism, Christianity, Orthodox churches, the Church of the Holy Sepulcher, and Islam.

Jerusalem is synonymous with the birth and life of Jesus on earth. There are two accounts of Jerusalem in the Bible: one is earthly Jerusalem, the "Holy Land," which Prophet Isaiah wrote about in his prophecy:

> *"Arise, Jerusalem! Let your light shine for all to see, for the glory of the Lord rises to shine on you. Darkness as black as night covers all the nations of the earth, but the glory of the Lord rises and appears over you. All nations will come to your light, and mighty kings will come to see your radiance... At the right time, I, the Lord, will make it happen."*

> **— *Isaiah 60:1-22 (NLT)***

The second is the "New Jerusalem," promised to saints through the vision of Apostle John, revealed by the Lord's angels in the book of Revelation:

> *"Then I saw a new heaven and a new earth, for the old heaven and the old earth had disappeared. And the sea was also gone. And I saw the Holy City, the New Jerusalem, coming down from God out of heaven like a bride beautifully dressed for her husband."*

> **— *Revelation 21:1-2 (NLT)***

The city of Jerusalem is the "heartthrob" of Israel, the Holy Land, and the epicenter of the nation. It is laid out in such a way that the Mount of Olives overlooks the Holy City.

To the left is the Garden of Gethsemane, and to the right is the Church of All Nations. The two roads on either side lead to Bethany, through which Jesus entered Jerusalem.

Jesus lamented over the sins of Jerusalem several times:

"O Jerusalem, Jerusalem, killing the prophets and those who are sent to you! How often would I have gathered your children together as a hen gathers her brood under her wings, and you would not!"

— *Matthew 23:37 and Luke 13:34 (NKJV)*

CHAPTER TWO

THE GENEALOGY OF JESUS CHRIST

"When she brought forth, she sent to her father-in-law, saying, 'By the man whose these are, am I with child.' And she said, 'Discern, I pray thee, whose are these, the signet, and bracelets, and staff.'"

— Genesis 38:25

The genealogy of Jesus Christ is dramatic, satirically engulfed in dysfunction, tribulation, and triumph. However, the first "Hebrew" must have come out of an unresolved history. Many scholars have sought to resolve this mystery. Rabbi Lavinger wrote:

"'Hebrew' may have come from Eber, changed through the years to Ibri or Ibrim. But whether this was the Biblical Eber, a descendant of Shem, son of Noah, or

from the word 'Eber,' meaning 'From across the river,' is not known. The first is likely since from Shem, we also get the word Shemite or Semite."

— Rabbi Lee Levinger (The Story of the Jews)

The first Hebrews were among the settlers of cities created for God by man. Abraham was the son of Terah, who lived in Ur, a country in the land of the Chaldeans. God favored Abraham and asked him to leave his country for an unknown destination:

"Now the Lord had said unto Abram, 'Get thee out of thy country, and from thy kindred, and from thy father's house, unto a land that I will show thee. And I will bless them that bless thee, and curse him that curseth thee, and in thee shall all the families of the earth be blessed.'"

— Genesis 12:1-3 (NKJV)

This promise to Abram is the second covenanted agreement between man and God. This covenant is a prophetic declaration that mystifies the deity of God Almighty and the power of His sovereignty. Men and science are thrown into oblivion as they try to question the origin of life and the chronology of God's creation.

Jesus' genealogy not only resolves the questions of His unequivocal messiahship, deity, and role as Savior of the universe, but it also helps obliterate the myth of evolution.

God fulfilled His promise to Abraham through his children despite a prolonged battle with barrenness. Abraham and Sarah eventually had a child of promise, Isaac. The circumstances surrounding Isaac's pregnancy and birth caused pandemonium in the house of Abraham **(Genesis 21:1-24).**

Abraham's call to sacrifice Isaac and his obedience to God's command earned him the "Father of Faith" title. Abraham hit a home run and was given a flag of righteousness for his victory run, while his accolades (Christians) cheered on. What a victory for God's children and a revelation of Abraham's faithfulness **(Genesis 22:1-8).**

As soon as Abraham finished the offering, he called the name of the mountain "Jehovah-Jireh," as it is called to this day. There came the voice of an angel from heaven to Abraham:

> *"By myself have I sworn, saith the Lord, for because thou hast done this thing, and hast not withheld thy son, thine only son, that in blessing I will bless thee, and in multiplying, I will multiply thy seed as the stars of heaven and as the sand which is upon the seashore; and thy seed shall possess the gate of his enemies, and in thy seed shall all the nations of the earth be blessed because thou hast obeyed my voice."*
>
> *— **Genesis 22:16-18***

JACOB

There is a deeper meaning to the provision of the lamb for Abraham's sacrifice instead of his only son of promise, Isaac. This was God's way of letting man know that He was done with the sacrifice of firstborns for fertility in Israel, no matter the tradition or religious obligation. Human blood is forever rejected for any kind of attainment.

Esau and Jacob were two sons of Isaac, but God favored the younger son to carry forward Isaac's legacy. Jacob had been chosen by God to be the third link in His plan for Abraham's lineage, becoming the father of the world. The name Jacob means "Supplanter," one who takes by force (by cheating). Jacob received his father's blessing, more or less a prophetic anointing as the heir apparent. Esau hated his brother Jacob and planned to kill him. But their parents sent him away:

> *"And Jacob obeyed his father and his mother and was gone to Padanaram."*
>
> **— *Genesis 28:7 (NKJV)***

Jacob went to his mother's brother, Laban, and married two of his daughters, Rachel and Leah. God blessed his marriages with twelve children. The twelve children of Jacob, along with his two grandsons, combined to become the twelve tribes of Israel as soon as God changed Jacob's name to Israel **(Genesis 29:29-35, 30:1-24)**.

Levinger, in his account of the Hebrews' twelve tribes, wrote:

> *"The Hebrews were divided into twelve tribes according to their descent from the sons of Jacob, who was called Israel. Reuben, Simeon, Levi, Judah, Issachar, and Zebulun were Jacob's children by Leah. Rachel's sons were Joseph and Benjamin. (One tribe was named for each of the two sons of Joseph, Ephraim, and Manasseh, so the actual count became thirteen). Gad, Asher, Dan, and Naphtali were children of the handmaidens, Zilpah and Bilhah. But all these tribes thought of themselves as the children of one father, Israel."*

Jacob is the third generation of Abraham. In fact, the history of his life and family is more chaotic and dysfunctional than that of his father, Isaac, and grandfather combined.

There is an old adage (proverb) from Africa that says, "A lion must give birth to a lion, not a dog." This means that children often portray the character of their parents. Jacob's grandfather, Abraham, was a class act, but he had character flaws that could have destroyed his family if not for the intervention of divine providence, mercy, and compassion from Almighty God. Abraham deceived King Abimelech and said:

> *"And Abraham said, 'Because I thought, surely the fear of God is not in this place, and they will slay me for my wife's sake. And yet indeed she is my sister; she is the daughter of my father, but not the daughter of my*

> *mother; and she became my wife. And it came to pass, when God caused me to wander from my father's house, that I said to her, This is thy kindness which thou shalt shew unto me; at every place whither we shall come, say of me, He is my brother.'"*

— Genesis 20:11-13 (KJV)

Abraham planted some bad seeds in his family, and they followed his descendants.

This raises a conscious question for every Christian and believer: What kind of seeds are we planting in our lives and families? These may germinate and bear generational resemblance in our children. May God forbid!

Secondly, Father Abraham was involved in an adulterous relationship with his maidservant, Hagar. This relationship resulted in the birth of Ishmael. Regardless of the fact that Sarah initiated the "Hollywood" drama—writing and directing the scenes—Abraham was overwhelmed and flabbergasted. He misjudged God's master plan for his life. Abraham and Sarah are not alone in this abstentious parallel life drama. As you read this passage, can you identify where you have missed the mark, like Abraham and Sarah?

The Spirit of the Lord is saying it's not too late. It's always better to be late than delayed. Repent and ask God for forgiveness. "Just do it." Make a turn in the right direction and save your life. Here are Paul's edifying words to the Ephesians:

"Finally, my brethren, be strong in the Lord and in the power of His might. Put on the whole armor of God, that ye may be able to stand against the wiles of the devil. For we wrestle not against flesh and blood, but against principalities, against powers, against the rulers of the darkness of this world, against spiritual wickedness in high places. Wherefore, take unto you the whole armor of God, that ye may be able to withstand in the evil day, and having done all, to stand. Stand, therefore, having your loins girt about with truth and having on the breastplate of righteousness."

— *Ephesians 6:10-20*

Jacob is the most significant "child of promise" among all of Abraham's descendants, not because of his character, power, or wisdom, but because he was a chosen, designated heir of Abraham to fulfill the covenant promises of God to Abraham:

"I will make of thee a great nation."

— *Genesis 12:2*

Jacob was a child of tribulation, perseverance, and triumph. He was a twin with Esau. In fact, Jacob was anointed in his mother's womb, Rebecca. Here is Moses' account of Esau and Jacob:

> *"And the children struggled together within her, and she said, 'If it be so, why am I thus?' And she went to inquire of the Lord. The Lord said unto her, 'Two nations are in thy womb, and two manner of people shall be separated from thy bowels; and the one people shall be stronger than the other people, and the elder shall serve the younger.'"*

— *Genesis 25:22-23 (KJV)*

Jacob made many mistakes in life due to his selfish choices and not waiting upon the Lord, like his grandfather Abraham. However, God had already chosen him and would not let go, regardless of his bad decisions. On Jacob's way to Laban, trying to escape from his brother Esau, God established His covenant plan with him:

> *"And, behold, I am with thee, and will keep thee in all places whither thou goest, and will bring thee again into this land; for I will not leave thee until I have done that which I have spoken to thee of."*

— *Genesis 28:15 (KJV)*

Here is a marvelous revelation of God's sovereignty. God is not a respecter of persons. He chooses His elect and anoints them for His glory. This shows that God can use anyone, regardless of their character or background, just as He used Paul, David, and other shepherds in Scripture. What an audacity of hope for every child of God! Are you available? Should God decide to knock on your door, remember it is not by your efforts or righteousness. Pray that God will use you and your talents for the end-time harvest.

JOSEPH: ANOTHER CHILD OF PROMISE IN THE HOUSE OF JACOB

Joseph was one of the two sons of Rachel, the daughter of Laban. After a prolonged period of barrenness, much like her mother-in-law Rebecca, God answered Rachel's prayers and blessed her with two sons, Joseph and Benjamin. She didn't have to earn Jacob's love by bearing children; Jacob already had a degree of unconditional "Agape Love" for her. However, we reserve the ultimate spirit and gratitude of honor for "Agape Love" to God Almighty.

It is of great interest to note that the genealogy of Jesus Christ creates and generates diverse interest in proving His credentials as the Messiah. The questions arise: (1) Is He truly from the Messianic Davidic ancestry? and (2) Can we clear the doubts and conflict surrounding the virgin birth of Jesus?

The birth of Jesus was as dramatic as that of His predecessors, Isaac and Jacob (Isaac: Genesis 21:1-34; Jacob: Genesis 30:1-42). Yet God had predestined Him as the fourth in the lineage of His prophetic Divine plan, Abraham's covenant for a great nation.

The God of the universe, and the God of the Jews, is a God of history. He has set the entire earth through His great handiwork of creation—Adam as the first parent of all life, and through Seth, Noah, and Abraham to David. God's plans and every one of His covenant plans with man must prevail and will come to pass.

Therefore, the genealogy of Jesus is a true revelation of the audacity of the Son—the Lamb, the Lion, the Messiah—and His mission, Jesus Christ. As you continue to read this book, you will realize that revelation leads to discovery, and discovery will lead to recovery. It is my desire as the author that this study will lead all my readers to discover their losses in life, which are a result of a lack of knowledge of Jesus Christ and His manifesto. At the same time, it will help redirect and provide a route to change in order to maximize your potential in life.

Joseph's life potential was discovered in Egypt through affliction, which led him to jail for three years. The revelation of his own dreams and those of others led to the discovery of his divine potential—the interpretation of dreams for the chief butler and the chief baker. One day, Pharaoh had a strange dream, and no one in his cabinet or country could interpret it except Joseph:

> *"Then Pharaoh sent and called Joseph, and they brought him hastily out of the dungeon. He shaved himself, changed his raiment, and came unto Pharaoh. Pharaoh said unto Joseph, 'I have dreamt a dream, and there is none that can interpret it. I have heard it said of thee, that thou canst understand dreams to interpret them.' And Joseph answered, saying, 'It is not in me; God shall give Pharaoh an answer of peace.'"*

— ***Genesis 41:14-16 (KJV)***

The discovery of Joseph's potential resulted in abundance, family prosperity, and a generational breakthrough for Israel, as well as Egypt's ability to withstand famine for seven years.

Pharaoh appointed Joseph as the governor of Egypt. The scripture presents this encounter as follows:

> *"Pharaoh said to Joseph, 'I hereby put you in charge of the whole land of Egypt.' Then Pharaoh took his signet ring from his finger and put it on Joseph's finger. He dressed him in robes of fine linen and put a gold chain around his neck. He had him ride in a chariot as his second-in-command, and men shouted before him, 'Make way!' Thus he put him in charge of the whole land of Egypt. Pharaoh said to Joseph, 'I am Pharaoh, but without your word, no one will lift a hand or foot in all Egypt.'"*

— *Genesis 41:41-44*

The story of Joseph is often compared to a "Hollywood movie script," directed by Arnold Schwarzenegger on steroids—dramatic but with a happy ending that captivated its audience. Joseph's brothers hated him; they were jealous of his dreams and the love bestowed on him by their father. They planned evil and tried to kill him, but God had a different agenda and a good plan for him:

> *"And when they saw him afar off, even before he came near unto them, they conspired against him to slay him. 'Let us cast him into some pit,' they said, 'and we will say some evil beast has devoured him, and we shall see what will become of his dreams.'"*

— *Genesis 37:18-20 (KJV)*

Many of us can relate to this story at one time or another. The good news is that God has good plans for all His children. We, as children of God, must believe and have faith in God's promises, for He rewards those who diligently love and seek Him.

The children of Israel came to Egypt to buy food, and Joseph revealed himself to his brothers:

> *"And Joseph said unto his brethren, 'Come near to me, I pray you.' And they came near. He said, 'I am Joseph, your brother, whom you sold into Egypt. Now, therefore, be not grieved nor angry with yourselves that you sold me hither, for God did send me before you to preserve life.'"*

— *Genesis 45:45 (NKJV)*

Joseph was blessed by God, rising from a slave to a great ruler in the land of his enslavement, Egypt. His wife was Asenath, and his two sons were Manasseh and Ephraim. The name of his first son, Manasseh, means "God has let me forget all my troubles." The second son, Ephraim, means "God has made me a success in the land of my troubles."

These two names, Manasseh and Ephraim, held spiritual significance for Joseph. He discovered the ministry of forgiveness, as the Psalmist wrote:

> *"Blessed is he whose transgression is forgiven, whose sin is covered. Blessed is the man unto whom the Lord imputeth not iniquity, and in whose spirit there is no guile."*
>
> *— **Psalms 32:1-2 (KJV)***

Joseph's forgiveness toward his brothers parallels Jesus' parable about the unforgiving debtor:

> *"Then his lord, after that he had called him, said unto him, 'O thou wicked servant, I forgave thee all thy debt because thou desirest me. Shouldest not thou also have had compassion on thy fellow servant, even as I had pity on thee?'"*
>
> *— **Matthew 18:32-33 (KJV)***

Joseph brought his family, servants, and Hebrew families to live in Egypt, and they inhabited the country of Goshen. The Hebrews prospered in Egypt as long as Joseph remained in the cabinet of the ruling Pharaoh. Here is the perspective of one of the Jewish writers, Levinger, who wrote:

> *"The Hebrews prospered there, as the story of Joseph tells, and served the Pharaoh faithfully and diligently, acting as a military buffer against invaders from the North and East. But the new Pharaoh feared the Hebrews' freedom and forgot their services. The Hebrew shepherds and*

> *farmers were forced to build monuments and storehouses to the glory of the Pharaoh. So a free, wider-roaming people were enslaved."*

— Levinger and Gersh (The Story of the Jew)

The Bible tells us that through the story of Joseph, we learn that afflictions and suffering help develop obedience, character, humility, and divine wisdom for leadership. In fact, the Israelites lived in Egypt for a period of 430 years (Exodus 12:40).

However, it is worthy to mention that Joseph had amazing faith. He believed in the return of the Israelites to the Promised Land, the land of Canaan. The Apostle Paul, in his epistle to the Hebrews, wrote:

> *"By faith Joseph, when he died, made mention of the departure of the children of Israel, and gave commandment concerning his bones."*

— Hebrews 11:22 (KJV)

Joseph was fully persuaded by the Lord God of his fathers—Jacob, Isaac, and Abraham. He was not moved by his ordeal with his brothers (Genesis 37:1-36) nor by the betrayal of Potiphar and his wife's accusation of rape (Genesis 39:1-19).

God was with Joseph, and he relied on the will and faithfulness of the Almighty God, just like the spiritual words of edification and encouragement from the Apostle Paul to the Romans:

> *"And we know that God causes everything to work together for the good of those who love God and are called according to his purpose for them. For God knew his people in advance and chose them to become like his Son."*
>
> *— **Romans 8:28-29 (NLT)***

JUDAH, THE SON OF JACOB

> *"Judah, thou art he whom thy brethren shall praise. Thy hand shall be in the neck of thine enemies; thy father's children shall bow down before thee. Judah is a lion's whelp: from the prey, my son, thou art gone up. He stooped down, he couched as a lion, and as an old lion; who shall rouse him up? The scepter shall not depart from Judah, nor a lawgiver from between his feet, until Shiloh comes, and unto him shall the gathering of the people be."*
>
> *— **Genesis 49:8-10 (KJV)***

Great leaders are born, not made. They stand out in times of challenges and adversity, exercising serenity, courage, wisdom, and inherent leadership gifts. Judah was the fourth of Jacob's twelve sons, and he exhibited outspoken leadership traits. Judah's father, Jacob, spiritually confirmed his leadership skills through prophetic blessings to all his children before his death. He prophesied over Judah:

> *"Judah, your brothers will praise you; you will grasp your enemies by the neck; all your relatives will bow before you. Judah, my son, is a young lion that has finished eating its prey. Like a lion, he crouches and lies down; like a lioness, who dares to rouse him? The scepter will not depart from Judah, nor the ruler's staff from his descendants, until the coming of the one to whom it belongs, the one whom all nations will honor."*

— *Genesis 49:8-10 (NLT)*

The story of Judah confirms that God predestined each of His children on earth. Judah, despite his leadership skills, had character flaws. Yet his father blessed him, and God chose him to be the father of Israel's lineage of kings, which would eventually produce the Messiah.

Let's examine some of Judah's attributes and his compassion during the adversity that confronted Joseph's brothers. When the decision arose whether to kill Joseph or throw him into the pit (Genesis 37:20-27), it was Judah who stood in the gap and exhibited Godly love and compassion. Judah responded:

> *"Come, let us sell him to the Ishmaelites, and let not our hand be upon him, for he is our brother and our flesh."*

— *Genesis 37:27 (KJV)*

In fact, when the "silver cup" that belonged to Joseph was found in Benjamin's bag, a dramatic situation unfolded. Judah rose to the occasion in defense of his brother Benjamin's innocence as the children of Israel were thrown into a state of confusion. Here is Judah's perspective:

> *"Governor Joseph demanded, 'What have you done? Don't you know that a man like me can predict the future?'"*

— Genesis 44:15

> *"Judah answered, 'Oh! My lord, what can we say to you? How can we explain this? How can we prove our innocence? God is punishing us for our sins. My lord, we have all returned to be your slaves—all of us, not just our brother who had your cup in his sack.'"*

— Genesis 44:16 (NLT)

> *"'No,' Joseph said. 'I would never do such a thing! Only the man who stole the cup will be my slave. The rest of you may go back to your father in peace.'"*

— Genesis 44:17

Then Judah stepped forward and said:

> *"'Please, my lord, let your servant say just one word to you. Please do not be angry with me, even though you are as powerful as Pharaoh himself. But you told us, unless your youngest brother comes with you, you will never see my face again.*

So we returned to your servant, our father, and told him what you said. We can't go unless you let our youngest brother go with us. Then our father said to us, "As you know, my wife had two sons, and one of them went away and never returned. Now, if you take his brother away from me and anything happens to him, you will send this grieving, white-haired man to the grave."

Our father's life is bound up in the boy's life; if he sees that the boy is not with us, our father will die. My lord, I guaranteed to take care of the boy. I told him, "If I don't bring him to you, I will bear the blame forever."

So, please, my lord, let me stay here as a slave instead of the boy and let the boy return with his brothers. For how can I return to my father if the boy is not with me? I can't bear the anguish this would cause my father."

— ***Genesis 44:17-33 (NLT)***

Looking at these events, we could postulate that God can use anyone, regardless of imperfections and sin. Reflecting on the lives of everyone in Jesus' genealogy, we can see their flaws and challenges.

Abraham lied and gave up his wife, Sarah, to King Abimelech, claiming she was his sister in exchange for food (Genesis 20:1). He also sent Ishmael and his mother, Hagar, away, which involved him in an adulterous relationship **(Genesis 21:9-11).**

Isaac, a child of promise, was a man of great patience and God-fearing, but he would lie rather than confront the truth. With human wisdom, one might call him a father of favoritism between his two sons, Esau and Jacob. This created division in his family rather than love. But one may ask: could this have been an orchestration of God's divine plan? We need divine wisdom for a conclusive answer.

Jacob, whose name means "Supplanter" (to take by force or replace), could have won an "Award" for a class act—a graduate honors degree in "Fraudology" at the University of Moron Lake. But for the love and mercy of God, and because he repented, God always opened His doors for His children to return.

Let's examine the words of the prophet Hosea:

"The Lord hath also a controversy with Judah, and will punish Jacob according to his doings; He will recompense him. He took his brother by the heel in the womb, and by his strength, he had power with God. Yea, he had power over the angel and prevailed; he wept and made supplication unto him. He found him in Bethel, and there He spake with us, even the Lord God of hosts; the Lord is His memorial."

— *Hosea 12:2-5 (KJV)*

The story of Judah is vast and intertwined with the life and ministry of Jesus Christ because of the prophetic words of his father, Jacob, and the prophets. The scepter has been cast upon his head and his roots, as foretold in Genesis:

> *"The scepter shall not depart from Judah, nor a lawgiver from between his feet, until Shiloh comes, and unto him shall the gathering of the people be."*
>
> — ***Genesis 49:10 (KJV)***

There are only two people in the Bible whose images have been likened to the character of a lion: Jesus and Judah. However, for clarity, this chapter will only address Judah's lion character. Judah never succumbed nor yielded his position in the face of adversity. His courageous, humble personality manifested regardless.

The Bible presents one of Judah's accountability challenges that probably helped shape his destiny—Judah's encounter with Tamar:

> *"Then Judah said to Tamar, his daughter-in-law, 'Go back to your parents' home and remain a widow until my son Shelah is old enough to marry you.' (But Judah didn't really intend to do this because he was afraid Shelah would also die, like his two brothers.) So Tamar went back to live in her father's home.*
>
> *Some years later, Judah's wife died. After the time of mourning was over, Judah and his friend Hirah the Adullamite went to Timnah to supervise the shearing of his sheep. Someone told Tamar, 'Look, your father-in-law is going up to Timnah to shear his sheep.' Tamar was aware that Shelah had grown up, but no arrangements had been made for her to marry him.*

So she changed out of her widow's clothing and covered herself with a veil to disguise herself. Then she sat beside the road at the entrance to the village of Enaim, which is on the road to Timnah. Judah noticed her and thought she was a prostitute since she had covered her face. So he stopped and propositioned her. 'Let me have sex with you,' he said, not realizing that she was his own daughter-in-law.

'How much will you pay to have sex with me?' Tamar asked.

'I will send a young goat from my flock,' Judah promised.

'But what will you give me to guarantee that you will send the goat?' she asked.

'What kind of guarantee do you want?' he replied.

She answered, 'Leave me your identification seal and its cord and the walking stick you are carrying.' So Judah gave them to her. Then, he had intercourse with her, and she became pregnant. Afterward, she went back home, took off her veil, and put on her widow's clothing as usual.

Later, Judah asked his friend, the Adullamite, to take the young goat to the woman and pick up the things he had given her as his guarantee. But Hirah couldn't find her. So he asked the men who lived there, 'Where can I find the shrine prostitute who was sitting beside the road at the entrance to Enaim?'

We've never had a shrine prostitute here,' they replied.

So Hirah returned to Judah and told him, 'I couldn't find her anywhere, and the men of the village claim they've never had a shrine prostitute there.'

'Then let her keep the things I gave her,' Judah said. 'I sent the young goat as we agreed, but you couldn't find her. We'd be the laughingstock of the village if we went back again to look for her.'

About three months later, Judah was told, 'Tamar, your daughter-in-law, has acted like a prostitute. And now, because of this, she's pregnant.'

'Bring her out, and let her be burned!' Judah demanded.

But as they were taking her out to kill her, she sent this message to her father-in-law: 'The man who owns these things made me pregnant. Look closely. Whose seal and cord and walking stick are these?'

Judah recognized them immediately and said, 'She is more righteous than I am because I didn't arrange for her to marry my son Shelah.' And Judah never slept with Tamar again.

When the time came for Tamar to give birth, it was discovered that she was carrying twins. While she was in labor, one of the babies reached out his hand. The midwife grabbed it and tied a scarlet string around the child's wrist, announcing, 'This one came out first!' But he pulled back his hand, and then out came his brother!

'What!' the midwife exclaimed. 'How did you break out first?' So he was named Perez. Then the baby with the scarlet string on his wrist was born, and he was named Zerah."

— Genesis 38:11-29 (NLT)

This story of Judah and Tamar is complex, but Judah rose to the occasion and accepted the shame, the religious myth, and the demands and consequences. He declared, "She is more righteous than I am because I did not arrange for her to marry my son Shelah." **(Genesis 38:26)**

Many wealthy people in Israel would have executed Tamar to protect their royal class rather than absorb the shame and stand for the truth. Could this answer one of the questions this book will explore:

WHY DOES GOD USE AND PROMOTE SINFUL PEOPLE?

Despite Judah's manipulative spirit and his family's dysfunction, the great "Jesus," the Son, the Lamb, the Lion, the Messiah, and His Mission is a byproduct of this enigmatic son of Jacob, grandson of Isaac and Abraham, called Judah.

MOSES

> *"Finally, the king called in Shiphrah and Puah, the two women who helped the Hebrew mothers give birth (midwives). He told them, 'If a Hebrew woman gives birth to a girl, let the child live. If the baby is a boy, kill him.'"*
>
> **— *Exodus 2:15 (CEV)***

The name "Moses" was given by the daughter of the Egyptian Pharaoh, who found him in a basket left floating on the riverbank. "Moses" means "found in the river."

Now comes a great warrior, a prophet, a one-man army, a field marshal without a brigade or regiment, a grandson of Abraham, Isaac, and Jacob, from a Hebrew woman's reckless abandonment—Moses, left at the mercy and grace of Almighty God and predestination, in a basket by the riverbank.

Moses' parents must have exhausted all their options, yet the ethos of hope abided. Perhaps Moses' parents were right to invest their faith. Father James Keller wrote in *The Christopher's*:

- "Hope looks for the good in people instead of harping on the worst.

- Hope opens doors where despair closes them.

- Hope draws its power from a deep trust in God and the basic goodness of human nature.

- Hope 'lights a candle' instead of 'cursing the darkness.'

- Hope regards problems, small or large, as opportunities.

- Hope pushes ahead when it would be easy to quit.

- Hope is a good loser because it has the divine assurance of final victory."

Levinger and Gersh, in their study of the Jews, wrote:

"Moses (Thirteenth Century B.C.E.) was brought up as an Egyptian prince. In his youth, he lived a life of absolute luxury, surrounded by slaves, feasting, and riches of all kinds. But he gave up this life because he could not live with the accompanying sights and sounds of Egyptian injustice and brutality.

Moses fled into the wilderness, finding peace in the life of a shepherd. There, in the loneliness of the desert, God's voice bade Moses return to Egypt and lead His people, the Hebrews, to freedom. Armed only with the Word of God, Moses faced the might of Pharaoh. It was enough."

The children of Israel sojourned in the land of Goshen when they joined Joseph in Egypt. They remained in Goshen as their homeland for a period of 400 years. God prospered them, and they grew substantially, maintaining their culture and religion as a separate community outside Egypt **(Genesis 47:5-6).**

The death of Joseph brought an awakening to both the Hebrews and the Egyptians. A new Pharaoh rose to power who did not know Joseph, nor did he acknowledge Joseph's legacy and all the efforts and development brought to Egypt by Joseph's leadership during the famine **(Exodus 1:8-10)**. This new Pharaoh enslaved the people of Israel:

> *"Now there arose up a king who knew not Joseph. And he said unto his people, 'Behold, the people of Israel are more and mightier than we. Come on, let us deal wisely with them, lest they multiply, and it comes to pass that, when there falleth out any war, they also join unto our enemies and fight against us, and so get up out of the land.'"*

— Exodus 1:8-10 (KJV)

As a result of this double jeopardy, the Israelites became victims of fate and circumstance. The Egyptians subjected them to hard labor and oppressed them to a deplorable state. The Israelites became overwhelmed and intolerable. However, they lamented and cried out to the God of their ancestors for help. They believed in the one God of their fathers—Abraham, Isaac, and Jacob. And the Almighty God responded to their prayers. What was the result?

A mighty warrior, a generational leader, and an extraordinary prophet entered the scene. Moses, the handsome young man **(Exodus 2:2),** was born to Levite parents. This was the confirmation of the prophetic Levites' priesthood to be established through the law in the Promised Land.

Moses is a seed of a fig tree planted by Levite parents by the riverbanks, which was harvested by Pharaoh's daughter to prepare a special meal to sustain her enemies, the Israelites! What a divine plan to fulfill a divine promise to Abraham and his generation **(Genesis).**

The story of Moses seems like an American Hollywood reality movie, but it is a true story that took place in the thirteenth century, B.C.E. Moses, as a prophet and leader, was predestined and ordained by God to lead the people of Israel out of slavery in the hands of the Egyptians.

> *"One day, as Moses led the sheep and goats of his father-in-law Jethro, the priest of Midian, across the desert to Sinai, to the holy mountain, he saw a burning bush that was not consumed by the fire. He drew nearer to the scene, curious.*
>
> *The Angel of the Lord appeared to him from the fire and called, 'Moses!'*
>
> *He answered, 'Here I am.'*
>
> *God replied, 'Don't come any closer. Take off your sandals, for the ground where you are standing is holy. I am the God who was worshipped by your ancestors, Abraham, Isaac, and Jacob.'*
>
> *Moses was afraid to look at God, so he hid his face.*

The Lord said, 'I have seen how my people are suffering as slaves in Egypt, and I have heard them beg for my help because of the way they are being mistreated. I feel sorry for them, and I have come down to rescue them from the Egyptians. I will bring my people out of Egypt into a country where there is good land rich with milk and honey. I will give them the land where the Canaanites, Hittites, Amorites, and Perizzites live. I am sending you to lead my people out of this country.'

But Moses said, 'Who am I to go to the king and lead your people out of Egypt?'

God replied, 'I will be with you, and you will know that I am the one who sent you when you worship me on this mountain after you have led my people out of Egypt.'

Moses answered, 'I will tell the people of Israel that the God their ancestors worshipped has sent me to them. But what should I say if they ask me your name?'

God said to Moses, 'I am the eternal God, so tell them that the Lord, whose name is "I AM," has sent you. This is my name forever, and it is the name that people must use from now on.'"

— Exodus 3:7-15 (CEV)

Let's look at a different interpretation of verses 14-15:

"And God said to Moses, 'I AM THAT I AM.' And He said, 'Thus shalt thou say unto the children of Israel, the Lord God of your fathers, the God of Abraham, the God of Isaac, and the God of Jacob, hath sent me unto you: this is my name forever, and this is my memorial unto all generations.'"

— *Exodus 3:14-15 (KJV)*

At the end of God's commission to Moses, He instructed Moses to go back to Egypt, gather the elders together, and say to them that God had ordered Moses and the elders to go to the king of Egypt to demand that he and his people let the children of Israel go to the mountains for three days to worship and sacrifice to the Lord their God.

And the Lord promised Moses:

"I will bring you out of the affliction of Egypt unto the land of the Canaanites, and Hittites, and Amorites, and Perizzites, and Jebusites, and the Hivites, unto a land flowing with milk and honey."

— *Exodus 3:17-18 (KJV)*

Exodus 3:7-18 marks and resonates with the commission of Moses by God to undertake a multi-catastrophic task, which American Hollywood would describe as a "Mission Impossible Thriller." But with God, this mission set out for Moses and Aaron is possible with God as the leader.

Moses, in verses 13-15, dialogued with God to know and ascertain which God was speaking to him. The children of Israel had multiple religions—some worshipped natural objects as gods, while others believed in the one and only God, the God of Abraham, Isaac, and Jacob, and their ancestors.

In Exodus 3:14, the Almighty God established His deity: "I AM THAT I AM," a God that is not seen or represented by a natural object. In Hebrew, the word "I AM THAT I AM" is JEHOVAH or YAHWEH. God reminded Moses of the covenant He made with his ancestors: Abraham (Genesis 12:1-17), Isaac (Genesis 26:2-5), and Jacob (Genesis 28:13-15).

The Almighty God refused to allow Moses' fears and excuses to stop Him from sending Moses to Pharaoh to demand the release of the children of Israel. Poor Moses—the audacious grip and divine assignment of God had fallen upon him. He could neither hide nor escape from this call to deliver his people from the wrath of the Egyptians.

Unlike Jonah, the prophet who dressed up in his Olympic-winner shoes and bolted to Tarshish **(Jonah 4:1-11),** Moses didn't try to run away. However, God forced Jonah to go to Nineveh to proclaim His message. And when Jonah planned another escape, God was more concerned with the spiritual well-being of 120,000 unbelieving Ninevites than the emotions of one prophet. So, God offered Jonah a free ride in the belly of a fish, which delivered him to Nineveh. The good news was that Jonah was healed of pride, and the people of Nineveh were delivered from destruction.

> *"Moses' attitude toward God set him apart from the children of Israel. Moses hungered for God. He delighted in His ways and word. The first time God manifested Himself to Moses as the great fire in the bush, Moses responded, 'I will turn aside and see this great sight."*

— *Exodus 3:3*

From that time on, God was his life and constant pursuit. God was the force of Moses' heart, whether God met him on the mountain or in the tabernacle of meeting."

Finally, Moses gathered his family from the house of his father-in-law, Jethro, and headed back to Egypt. Before Moses returned from Midian to Egypt, God said to him:

> *"Return to Egypt, for all those who wanted to kill you have died."*

— *Exodus 4:19 (NLT)*

God instructed Moses to go to Pharaoh immediately upon his arrival in Egypt to ask for the release of the children of Israel, accompanied by the elders of Israel. God told Moses:

> *"As you go to Pharaoh, perform all the miracles I have empowered you to do. But I will harden his heart so he will refuse to let the people go. Then you will tell him:*

> *'This is what the Lord says: Israel is my firstborn son. Let my son go so he can worship me. But since you have refused, I will now kill your firstborn son.'*

— ***Exodus 4:21-23 (NLT)***

The story of the Israelites and their enslavement has attracted much interest and study. Let's examine Connick's perspective concerning Moses, the elders of Israel, and Pharaoh:

> *"That wily tyrant, Pharaoh, flatly refused to submit to Moses' demands for three work-free days of worship. Instead, he increased the workload and withdrew the straw he had previously provided for brick-making. Crestfallen, Moses turned to the Lord, who empowered him to plague Pharaoh into submission.*
>
> *Moses had to count to ten before his efforts were crowned with success. Only when the angel of death passed over the Hebrews and struck down the firstborn of the Egyptians did Pharaoh yield. He told Moses to take his people with him, worship the Lord, and return. The Hebrews left (shortly after 1290 B.C.), but they had no intention of returning.*
>
> *Pharaoh's melting heart soon hardened, and he pursued them. The sea parted for Moses and his people, but it closed on the Egyptians.*

'Thus the Lord saved Israel that day... and the people feared the Lord, and they believed in His servant Moses.'"

— ***Exodus 14:30-31***

The Almighty God used His obedient servant Moses to deliver His people, Israel, from the land of their enslavement to freedom. The deliverance of Israel from bondage remains one of the greatest real stories, though it may seem like folklore, a reality show, or a fantasy fiction story to satirize humanity.

In contrast, we are about to uncover the true characteristics of "man." Moses was a true servant and prophet of God, and God was with him. He was both highly spirited and, at the same time, human. He made mistakes, and pride got in the way as the children of Israel headed to Mount Sinai. The children of Israel were challenged, and the scarcity of food and water caused their faith to erode. They became disillusioned instead of grateful for their freedom. Their disillusionment created havoc and leadership challenges for Moses and Aaron.

The implications are that Moses and Aaron were overwhelmed, and they failed to follow God's instructions. The children of Israel fell victim to disobedience to God and His commandments. But God's grace and covenant remain forever. God spoke through the prophet Isaiah:

> *"Arise, shine, for your light has come, and the glory of the Lord is risen upon you. For behold, the darkness shall cover the earth, and deep darkness the people, but the Lord will arise over you, and His glory will be seen upon you. The Gentiles shall come to your light, and kings to the brightness of your rising."*

— *Isaiah 60:1-3 (NKJV)*

The Word of God can't return to Him empty. These prophetic words, spoken by God through Isaiah, came to pass within a short time.

The glory of God was restored at Mount Sinai to those who repented and fervently waited for God. Our Almighty God is a just God, and He holds us accountable through His judgments. Moses and Aaron paid a costly price for disobeying God.

However, the fulfillment of bringing the children of Israel to Canaan had to come to pass, so God chose another leader, Joshua, for the continuation of the procession—the journey to the Promised Land. But God allowed Moses to help Joshua transition Israel to Canaan.

In fact, Moses was the prelude for the readiness and final concerning of the Holy Land. Moses was the mediator between the Israelites and God in establishing His commandments and laws that helped Joshua deliver the Israelites to Canaan. Moses remains a special jewel in the eyes of God and in the history of the Hebrews.

Now, let's look at what happened to the children of Israel as they crossed the Red Sea. God allowed all the adult children of Israel to be enrolled at the "University of Obedience," located in the wilderness of Shur. The two courses were *Psychology of Murmuring 101* and *Psychology of Rebellion 102*.

In fact, to Moses and Aaron's surprise, the entire adult population of Israel flunked *Psychology of Murmuring 101* with F-grades. Moses, shocked and mesmerized, rose to the occasion. He put on his compassionate cap and went to God to plead for the children of Israel to retake the class:

> *"Then Moses led the people of Israel away from the Red Sea, and they moved out into the desert of Shur. They traveled in the desert for three days without finding any water. When they came to the oasis of Marah, the water was too bitter to drink. So they called the place Marah (which means 'bitter'). Then, the people complained and turned against Moses. 'What are we going to drink?' they demanded.*
>
> *So Moses cried out to the Lord for help, and the Lord showed him a piece of wood. Moses threw it into the water, and this made the water good to drink."*

— *Exodus 15:22-25 (NLT)*

In fact, it was not more than fifteen days after they left Marah for Elim and Mount Sinai that the children of Israel after God allowed them to retake *Psychology of Murmuring 101*, which they passed, failed *Psychology of Rebellion 102* with reckless abandon.

The entire community demanded the heads of Moses and Aaron. They cried and complained to them. Here is what they said:

> *"If only the Lord had killed us back in Egypt," they moaned. "There we sat around pots filled with meat and ate all the bread we wanted. But now you have brought us into this wilderness to starve us all to death!"*

— *Exodus 16:3 (NLT)*

But God heard their cries and provided the children of Israel with manna and quail from heaven, which they ate and were filled **(Exodus 16:1-12)**.

Moses was a prophet of many accomplishments: a Jewish leader, lawgiver, recorder of the Ten Commandments, and the author of the Pentateuch. He was a great man of God, but despite all his faith and obedience, Moses lacked spiritual discipline and leadership skills. He was human, married to Zipporah, the daughter of Jethro, the priest of Midian. He had a sister named Miriam, a brother, Aaron, and two sons, Gershom and Eliezer.

His lack of spiritual discipline resulted in his failure to enter the Promised Land of Canaan. Every leader called by God faces or will face challenges in pursuit of their mission and ministry. But our faithful God is full of mercy and providence. God knows our flaws and has already provided ready mentors and accountability partners to assist us through our journey. But are we willing to listen and search for angelic helpers around us? (Food for thought.)

In Moses' case, God had one readily available, and his name was "Reverend Priest Jethro" (food for thought).

This is one reason why some married men should stop seeing their fathers-in-law as obstacles. Instead, we should ask God to reveal the potential of every promising father-in-law—oops!

> *"Pastor Jethro," Moses' father-in-law, had wisdom and leadership skills that helped Moses mobilize and trust the people of Israel to help manage the human resources needed to deliver Israel to the Promised Land.*
>
> *And Jethro said to Moses, "Why do you let these people crowd around you from morning till evening?"*
>
> *Moses answered, "Because they come here to find out what God wants them to do. They bring their complaints to me, and I make decisions on the basis of God's law."*
>
> *Jethro replied, "That isn't the best way to do it. You and the people who come to you will soon wear out. The job is too much for one person; you can't do it alone. God will help you if you follow my advice. You should be the one to speak to God for the people, and you should teach them God's laws and show them what they must do to live right.*

> *You need to appoint some competent leaders who respect God and are trustworthy and honest. Then, put them in groups of ten, fifty, a hundred, and a thousand. These judges can handle ordinary cases and bring the more difficult cases to you. Having them share the load will make your work easier."*
>
> **— *Exodus 18:14-22 (CEV)***

Prophet Moses was the greatest leader of his people, Israel (Jews), and a shepherd of God's flock. His legacy lives forever. Apostle Stephen's last speech (Acts 7:20-43) commented on Moses' commission by God. And Apostle Paul also reflected on the character of God's servant Moses:

> *"By faith Moses, when he was come to years, refused to be called the son of Pharaoh's daughter, choosing rather to suffer affliction with the people of God than to enjoy the pleasures of sin for a season."*
>
> **— *Hebrews 11:24-25 (KJV)***

JOSHUA

> *"I brought you out of Egypt into this land that I swore to give your ancestors and said I would never break my covenant with you. For your part, you were not to make any covenants with the people living in your land; instead, you were to destroy their altars. But you didn't obey my command. Why did you do this?*

So now I declare that I will no longer drive out the people living in your land. They will be thorns in your sides, and their gods will be a constant temptation to you."

— *Judges 2:1-3 (NLT)*

As we continue to dig deeper into this study—*The Passion and Mission of Jesus Christ, the Messiah*—it becomes imperative to reflect on the introduction of the book:

"A journey of divine wisdom to 'Change' for abundant life and the eternal Kingdom."

This evokes the spirit of character accountability and responsibility for every child of God and those who seek to know Him. If read and absorbed diligently, this book will help readers change and understand that "change leads to discovery, and discovery results in recovery" in every human endeavor.

As Stanley F. Charles wrote:

"As we dig into God's Word, we learn who He is—His heart, His character, His will. We recognize the wisdom of obeying our Heavenly Father, not just because of the promised blessing, but because He knows what's best and loves us."

Moses' experience, a lesson in obedience, was the icing on the cake—a game changer for Joshua and the children of Israel regarding the task ahead. He made sure to impart his successor, Joshua, with the wisdom, will, and character of God, along with His covenant and demand for obedience. This was the only way to lead the children of Israel to Canaan.

> *"Therefore, obey the terms of this covenant so that you will prosper in everything you do. All of you—tribal leaders, elders, officers, and all the men of Israel—are standing today in the presence of the Lord your God. Your little ones and your wives are with you, as well as the foreigners living among you who chop your wood and carry water. You are standing here today to enter into the covenant of the Lord your God."*
>
> **— *Deuteronomy 29:9-12 (NLT)***

The passion for obeying God comes through character development and the challenges that lead to passionate submission to the commands and will of God. Absolute submission and commitment develop slowly through life experiences, failures, and trials. Not obeying God or disobedience has many consequences, tribulations, and sufferings. However, as believers and children of promise, the Apostle Paul charged the Romans and all children of inheritance to focus on what lies ahead—the future glory. Paul wrote:

> *"For we know that all creation looks forward to the day when it will join God's children in glorious freedom from death and decay. For we know that all creation has been groaning as in the pains of childbirth right up to the present time. And we believers also groan, even though we have the Holy Spirit within us as a foretaste of future glory, for we long for our bodies to be released from sin and suffering."*
>
> **— *Romans 8:22-23 (NLT)***

God wants the best for those who obey, submit, and wait for His will to be fulfilled. The children of Israel, as we discover, lacked character despite God's faithfulness and the glory He showed them. Their disobedience resulted in a 40-year delay and many deaths during their journey to Canaan. Faced with their circumstances and the plights of new believers, one may ask:

"WHAT DOES GOD WANT?"

The people of Israel and the people of the world today have one thing in common: their DNA is embedded in sin, and our DNA is similar to theirs. We are the heirs of Abraham.

Therefore, God's demands for humanity have not changed. God demands that all His creation be faithful, worship Him, and praise Him for His glory. As it says in Romans:

"God accepted Abraham because of his faith in Him."

— *Romans 4:3 (CEV)*

Our God is jealous and angry when we disobey His laws and commandments. But the love and blessings of God extend to everyone who loves and obeys His commands in faith:

"God promised Abraham many descendants. And when it all seemed hopeless, Abraham still had faith in God and became the ancestor of many nations. Abraham's faith never weakened, not even when he was nearly a hundred years old."

Joshua was able to transition from the shortcomings of Moses, the great leader, to recovery. God spoke through Moses to warn Joshua to listen, change, and choose life rather than death. Life and death decisions are very big responsibilities.

God never wanted the children of Israel to perish, so in His providence, He provided all His children with abundant life and prosperity but with the freedom to choose. As Moses said:

> *"Now listen! Today, I am giving you a choice between life and death, between prosperity and disaster, for I command you this day to love the Lord your God and to keep His commandments, decrees, and regulations by walking in His ways. If you do this, you will live and multiply, and the Lord your God will bless you and the land you are about to enter and occupy. But if your heart turns away and you refuse to listen, and if you are drawn away to serve and worship other gods, then I warn you now that you will certainly be destroyed."*
>
> **— *Deuteronomy 30:15-18 (NLT)***

Field Marshal Joshua had a very solid foundation, unlike Moses, whose circumstances left him at the riverbank in a basket, where he started his career as a loner and graduated in the wilderness as a wanderer. He completed his postgraduate studies at Mount Sinai with honors in "Sheepology." But it was only by God's grace that Moses' destiny was fulfilled. God discovered him, redeemed him, and led him to fulfill the calling of God upon his life. What a glorious display of God's providence.

Joshua became a master war strategist, decoding enemy attack plans and launching victory combats that led the Israelites into their God-given homeland. Moses was his mentor and teacher, and God was their Jehovah-Jireh—their provider. The exodus from Egypt to the Promised Land was divinely orchestrated by God under the dispensation of Abraham's descendants.

Joshua was a corporate, God-fearing leader in Israel, commissioned by the Lord as an ambassador through the great leader "General Moses." These two men, with the help of Aaron, Caleb, and Miriam, made the Exodus possible. Let's examine this verse, and perhaps the spirit of corporate leadership and divine connection may resonate with your spirit:

> *"And Moses did as the Lord commanded him: he took Joshua and set him before Eleazar, the priest, and before all the congregation. He laid his hands upon him and gave him a charge, as the Lord commanded by the hand of Moses."*
>
> — ***Numbers 27:22-23 (NKJV)***

After forty years of the children of Israel wandering in the wilderness, Moses brought them to the border of Canaan, with Joshua as his military captain. Only Joshua and Caleb, among the original Hebrews who marched out of Egyptian slavery, were able to enter the Promised Land. All the others who had suffered hard labor and enslavement died in the wilderness as they struggled to reach Canaan.

Levinger and Gersh summarized Joshua's leadership in their book *The Story of the Jews*. Here is their perspective:

"From that time until the establishment of the kingdom of Israel under Saul, a period of about two hundred years, the Israelites were governed by judges. Joshua was the first judge. Each tribe lived on its own land and governed its own affairs. Although they were one people, descended from Abraham, Isaac, and Jacob, and followed one God, the tribes did not act as one nation. Even when a great emergency required unity and a great leader rallied them, they were more often divided than united."

— *Levinger and Gersh, p. 22*

Joshua is described as a mighty commander and soldier with "double spirits." He had the human spirit of a gladiator and was never scared or afraid of any battle. He also had a godly combatant spirit, as he understood the faithfulness and power of the Almighty God behind him. Here is a biblical account of his conquest:

"So Joshua took all that land: the hills, all the south country, all the land of Goshen, the valley, the plain, the mountain of Israel, and the valley of the same, even from Mount Halak, that goes up to Seir, even unto Baal-gad in the valley of Lebanon under Mount Hermon. And all their kings he took, and smote them, and slew them.

Joshua made war a long time with all those kings. There was not a city that made peace with the children of Israel except the Hivites, the inhabitants of Gibeon. All the others they took in battle. For it was of the Lord to harden their hearts, that they should come against Israel in battle, that He might destroy them utterly, and that they might have no favor, but that He might destroy them, as the Lord commanded Moses."

— *Joshua 11:16-20 (NKJV)*

Joshua was God's "Ambassador extraordinary"; he was bestowed with divine wisdom, power, and the spirit of courage. Let's reflect on the Lord's words, charging Joshua's spirit to take the land of Canaan:

"Be strong and courageous, for you are the one who will lead these people to possess all the land I swore to their ancestors I would give them.

Be strong and very courageous. Be careful to obey all the instructions Moses gave you. Do not deviate from them, turning either to the right or to the left. Then, you will be successful in everything you do.

> *Study this Book of Instruction continually. Meditate on it day and night so you will be sure to obey everything written in it. Only then will you prosper and succeed in all you do.*
>
> *This is my command—be strong and courageous! Do not be afraid or discouraged. For the Lord your God is with you wherever you go."*
>
> ### *— Joshua 1:6-9 (NLT)*

"Faith begets courage, and courage begets obedience and confidence." Are you able to identify and relate to the words "BE STRONG AND COURAGEOUS"? How many times did God repeat them in this passage?

Anytime a word or statement is repeated in the Bible, twice or thrice, it represents a re-emphasized command with obligatory repercussions. God is sovereign, so He knows the heart of His son Joshua. He knows Joshua will be trustworthy for this assignment. But every servant of God will be tested.

What about you? What assignment does God have for you to do? Can you be found trustworthy? Will you be diligent and faithful in this assignment?

> *"God keeps His promise, and He will not allow you to be tested beyond your power to remain firm; at the time you are put to the test, He will give you the strength to endure it and so provide you with a way out."*
>
> ### *— 1 Corinthians 10:13 (TEV)*

As you read this book, the Spirit of God will resonate with every lost vision, dream, and assignment that the enemy (Satan) has stolen or distracted you from. Be strong and courageous, and know that the Lord God is with you. Most of God's assignments come with challenges and rewards. Always remember that perseverance in every assignment, with self-control, leads to success.

Rick Warren wrote in his book *The Purpose Driven Life*:

"Life on earth is a trust. This is the second metaphor of life. Our time on earth and our energy, intelligence, opportunities, relationships, and resources are all gifts from God that He has entrusted to our care and management. We are stewards of whatever God gives us. The concept of stewardship begins with the recognition that God is the owner of everything and everyone on earth."

Joshua delivered the children of Israel from the banks of the Jordan to the Promised Land of Canaan as the Word of God came to pass. God is in the business of deliverance, healing, and restoration. Hear God's Words to Jeremiah:

"No longer will they teach their neighbor or say to one another, 'Know the Lord,' because they will all know me, from the least of them to the greatest," declares the Lord.

— *Jeremiah 31:34 (NIV)*

THE JUDGES:

- Samuel
- Deborah
- Gideon
- Samson
- Saul

"...A system of judges was set up, and they were ordered not to pervert justice, not to show partiality to persons of title and wealth, and not to take gifts, for a gift blinds the eyes of the wise and perverts the words of the righteous."

— Levinger and Gersh, *The Story of the Jew*

From the end of Moses' dynasty to the establishment of Israel's kingdom, which lasted for about two hundred years, the Israelites were ruled by judges, and Joshua was the first judge. Joshua ensured that the Israelites kept the commandments and laws of God. But after Joshua's death, the Israelites were ruled and led by individual tribes. The tribes came together in times of emergency but maintained their differences as separate nations despite their common descent from Jacob, Isaac, and Abraham.

This generation of Israelites fell in love with the Canaanites, their lifestyle, and their gods, such as Baal. God was angry and sent an angel to Bokim to speak to the children of Israel:

"I brought you out of Egypt into this land that I swore to give your ancestors, and I said I would never break my covenant with you. For your part, you were not to make any covenants with the people living in this land. They will be thorns in your sides, and their gods will be constant temptations to you."

— Judges 2:1-2 (NLT)

From this time, God chose His leaders to lead the Israelites into battle. These elected leaders were called judges. Sisera, the commander of Jabin's army, made life in the land so miserable and intolerable for the Israelites that they cried out to God for help and redemption. Their condition of hopelessness lasted for twenty years. God appointed Deborah as a judge, and she presided over cases for the Israelites.

GIDEON

"But Lord," Gideon replied, "how can I rescue Israel? My clan is the weakest in the whole tribe of Manasseh, and I am the least in my entire family."

The Lord said to him, "I will be with you, and you will destroy the Midianites as if you were fighting against one man."

— Judges 6:15-16 (NLT)

The Israelites had sinned and disobeyed the Lord, God Almighty, and the Lord delivered the children of Israel into the hands of the Midianites **(Judges 6:1-6)**. The children cried out to God, and God commissioned Gideon through an angelic messenger to Gideon, the son of Joash, the Abiezrite. The angel of God appeared to Gideon and said to him:

> *"The Lord is with thee, thou mighty man of valor."*
>
> *And Gideon said unto him, "Oh, my Lord, if the Lord be with us, why then is all this befallen us? And where be all His miracles which our fathers told us of, saying, 'Did not the Lord bring us up from Egypt?' But now the Lord hath forsaken us and delivered us into the hands of the Midianites."*

— Judges 6:11-13 (NKJV)

Gideon, as mesmerized and delusional as he could be, somehow summoned the audacity to question the angel, asking, "If the Lord is with us, why has He forsaken us—the children of Israel?" Then the Lord Himself said:

> *"Gideon, you will be strong because I am giving you the power to rescue Israel from the Midianites... You can rescue Israel because I am going to help you. Defeating the Midianites will be as easy as beating up one man."*

— Judges 6:15-16 (NLT)

Gideon was a young man, full of life and wisdom. God knew him well enough for the angel to address him as "The Lord is with thee, thou mighty man of valor."

Let's pause here and explore the meaning of "valor." The Webster's Dictionary defines "valor" as exemplary courage, intrepidity, and bravery. The Lord, God, is omniscient, having infinite knowledge and knowing all things. He is also omnipotent.

God knew the heart of Gideon and his character. The call for stewardship is open and endless for every one of His children. We cannot outsmart God or avoid His obligations.

Are you ready and willing to accept the calling of God today? Peradventure, such a call comes suddenly. The Apostle Paul was a witness. Let's check these two verses and see how you can relate to his experiences and encouragements:

> *"I am sure that God, who began the good work within you, will keep right on helping you grow in His grace until His task within you is finally finished on that day when Jesus Christ returns."*

— Philippians 1:6 (LB)

> *"Work hard so you can present yourself to God and receive His approval. Be a good worker, one who does not need to be ashamed and who correctly explains the word of truth."*

— 2 Timothy 2:15 (NLT)

Gideon, the man of valor, was not hiding in shame or self-pity because of their circumstances. The Midianites had taken everything that belonged to the Israelites. Yet, there was an opportunity for the exhibition of God's gift for His purpose and glory. Gideon understood his purpose—attending to his father's business. Can we relate this to the two verses from the Apostle Paul, Philippians 1:6 and 2 Timothy 2:15? Gideon was busy with the little things:

> *"Joash's son Gideon was nearby threshing grain in a shallow pit, where he could not be seen by the Midianites."*

—Judges 6:11 (CEV)

Gideon was preparing grain and wheat to feed the other members of the family, fulfilling his ministry of service as empowered by God. Gideon questioned the angel and demanded proof and assurance that the calling was from the true God. Remember, the Canaanites worshiped many gods, and the children of God had become jealous and embraced their idol worship. Gideon, with his wisdom, said:

> *"It's hard to believe that I am actually talking to the Lord. Please do something so I will know that you really are the Lord. Wait here until I bring you an offering."*

> *"All right, I will wait," the Lord answered."*

Do you know that we worship an omnipresent God who is ready to talk and dialogue with you at any time? The story of Gideon will help you understand that God is in the relationship business. He is nearer than some of us think. Here's Gideon's tactic to prove that God's messenger was truly from the Lord. Gideon rushed home, killed a goat, boiled its meat, and prepared some bread and a pot of broth. He put them in a basket and brought them to the angel. Remember, the angel and God waited for Gideon to return. As he presented his offering to the angel under the tree, the angel ordered:

> *"Gideon, put the meat and the bread on the rock and pour the broth over them."*
>
> *Gideon did as he was told. The angel, holding a walking stick, touched the meat and bread with the end of the stick. Flames jumped from the rock and burned up the meat and bread."*

—Judges 6:15-21 (CEV)

As Gideon looked in surprise, he saw that the angel had disappeared. Fear gripped Gideon, and he thought he was going to die.

> *"The Lord replied, 'Calm down, Gideon; there is nothing to be afraid of. You are not going to die.'*
>
> *"Gideon built an altar to the Lord and worshiped, naming the place "The Lord Calms Our Fears."*

—Judges 6:23-24)

Gideon was an obedient servant of God's law and commandments. He understood the power of sacrifice under the first covenant with God. The sin sacrifice of animals was a part of God's commandment and covenant with Moses and the Israelites. These sacrifices were effective ways to appeal to the heart of God before the coming of Jesus and the new covenant.

For the people of Israel and their kings, animal sacrifices symbolized obedience and submission to God's law:

> *"...And the priest killed them, and made reconciliation with their blood (animals) upon the altar, to make an atonement for all Israel; for the king commanded that the burnt offering and the sin offerings should be made for all Israel."*
>
> **— 2 Chronicles 29:24 (KJV)**

God accepted Gideon's sacrifice as it was consumed by flames of fire. Gideon then went to war against the Midianites with his 300 soldiers, and God miraculously subdued the 135,000 Midianites at their hands. The trumpets and the pitchers became weapons of war, to the amazement of the children of Israel. Gideon had his limitations and fears, but God equips those He calls **(Judges 7:14-25).**

Rather than thanking God for His goodness, the people of Israel clung to Gideon, asking him to become their ruler. Gideon, however, was not confident in his capabilities despite God's backing and promises.

Gideon was a "Hall of Famer" in the Apostle Paul's list of "Faith Super Heroes" (Hebrews 11:32). But his character flaws resulted in unfaithfulness, and he failed to influence Israel to worship God. The children of Israel rallied around Gideon, demanding that he become their ruler and king. Lacking spiritual maturity, Gideon refused their offer, but then he led the Israelites into idol worship:

"Then the Israelites said to Gideon, 'Be our ruler! You and your son and your grandson will be our rulers, for you have rescued us from Midian.'

'I will not rule over you, nor will my sons; the Lord will rule over you. However, I do have one request: that each of you give me an earring from the plunder you collected from your enemies (the enemies being Ishmaelites, all of whom wore gold earrings).'

'Gladly,' they replied. They spread out a cloak, and each threw in a gold earring he had gathered from the plunder. Gideon made a sacred Ephod from the gold and put it in Ophrah, his hometown. But soon all the Israelites prostituted themselves by worshiping it, and it became a trap for Gideon and his family."

— *Judges 8:22-27 (NLT)*

SAMSON

"For lo, thou shalt conceive and bear a son, and no razor shall come on his head, for the child shall be a Nazarite unto God from the womb: and he shall begin to deliver Israel out of the hand of the Philistines."

— *Judges 13:5*

God calls and equips those He selects for His mission and purpose in life. In fact, let's examine the word "mission" in the Bible dictionary. Webster's dictionary defines the word *mission* as the act of sending or the state of being sent for a particular purpose; a diplomatic establishment in a foreign country; a force of specialists, scientists, etc., sent to a foreign country; and one's calling in life.

From Webster's definition, it's obvious that the word "mission" buttresses three allegorical senses:

- Action
- Purpose or Assignment
- Location

A mission conjures some covenant action and implications, which demand sacrifices at the altar of obedience. God is sovereign, and He equips everyone that He calls to serve—from Abraham, Isaac, and Jacob to Samson. They were men of valor with unique gifts and talents to subdue and bring their assignments to completion, as mandated by God's divine plan.

Secondly, every one of God's assignments is specific, inescapable, and sometimes inextricable from human wisdom or affluence. Thirdly, all of God's calls and assignments have directions, locations, and timing. And everyone called by God has the opportunity to prove His faithfulness and unleash the glory of His Almighty power.

One could ask, "How does God qualify those that He calls?" Men look at outward appearances while God searches the hearts of men. Here is the Word of God in Scripture to Samuel:

> *"Samuel, don't think Eliab is the one just because he's tall and handsome; he isn't the one I have chosen. People judge others by what they look like, but I judge people by what is in their heart."*

— *1 Samuel 16:7 (CEV)*

William James wrote, "The best use of life is to spend it for something that outlasts it." It would be exciting to know what every man—every steward—would like engraved on the marble of their tombstone. For me, it would be astonishing if only the dead could see "MISSION ACCOMPLISHED" on my tombstone, should God allow me to fulfill my mission on earth. What a wonderful feeling, a divine glory to our Heavenly Father, when the tolls are called, and there is an affirmation of assurance that our names are in the Book of Life.

I feel the breeze, the tranquility of the presence of the Holy Spirit. Do you feel the same? May our Almighty be praised. Another perspective from Rick Warren's book *The Purpose Driven Life* states:

> *"To fulfill your mission will require that you abandon your agenda and accept God's agenda for your life. You can't just 'tack it on' to all the other things you'd like to do with your life. You must say, like Jesus, 'Father… I want Your will, not mine.' You yield your rights, expectations, dreams, plans, and ambitions to Him… You hand God a blank sheet with your name signed at the bottom and tell Him to fill in the details."*

— **Rick Warren,** *The Purpose Driven Life*

Samson was called to deliver the children of Israel from the hands of the Philistines. His birth was dramatic and symphonic, similar to both the birth of his ancestor, Isaac and his predecessor, Jesus. These four births in the history of the Hebrews—if we add the birth of the forerunner of Jesus, John the Baptist—were divinely orchestrated and celebrated at the altar of predestination.

There was a man named Manoah and his wife from the land of Zorah. They were barren, and their house lacked both the noiseless pestilence of children and quasi-appointments to the pediatrician's office. And God remembered Manoah's wife, dedicating an angel to her. The angel said to her:

> *"Indeed now, you are barren and have borne no children, but you shall conceive and bear a son. Now, therefore, please be careful not to drink wine or eat anything unclean. For behold, you shall conceive and bear a son, and no razor shall come upon his head, for the child shall be a Nazarite to God from the womb, and he shall begin to deliver Israel out of the hand of the Philistines."*

—Judges 13:3-5

Here is a retrospect from Apostle Moses in Scripture:

> *"Then they (angels) said to him, 'Where is Sarah, your wife?' So he said, 'Here in the tent.' And He said, 'I will certainly return to you according to the time of life, and behold, Sarah, your wife, shall have a son.'"*

Genesis 18:8b-10 (NKJV)

Here is another prophetic birth announcement by an angel: the birth of John the Baptist. Zacharias, the priest, and his wife, Elizabeth, were righteous before God, but they were barren and well-advanced in age. One day, the Lord remembered him and his wife. The angel of the Lord appeared to him, standing on the right side of the altar of incense **(Luke 1:11)**. Zacharias was afraid and frightened:

> *"But the angel said to him, 'Do not be afraid, Zacharias, for your wife Elizabeth will bear you a son, and you shall call his name John.'"*

— *Luke 1:13 (NKJV)*

Now, the quadruple and echelon birth visitation by God's messenger, Angel Gabriel. However, in the sixth month, God sent His angel Gabriel to the city of Nazareth in Galilee, to a virgin named Mary, betrothed to Joseph. Heaven found Mary, and the angel said:

> *"…Rejoice, highly favored one, the Lord is with you; blessed are you among women!… Do not be afraid, Mary, for you have found favor with God. And behold, you will conceive in your womb and bring forth a son, and shall call His name Jesus."*

— *Luke 1:28b-31 (NKJV)*

These four divinely orchestrated births in the Bible had similar characteristics: a parallel denomination, family dysfunction, and glorious closures where God's faithfulness and victory triumphed over satanic forces.

Samson was born a Nazarite, dedicated to God at the altar of holiness, and divinely empowered to dethrone the Philistine army. In fact, Samson was so powerful that he was included in the Hebrew 11 Hall of Giants of Faith. However, he allowed the spirit of Delilah and Jezebel to handcuff him, shackling him to spiritual wisdom bankruptcy and a dungeon of self-deception.

Samson failed as a heroic judge with extraordinary strength, but he ultimately helped to rescue Israel from their oppression. Scripture records that Samson killed more Philistines on the day of his death than during his entire life:

> *"Then Samson called to the Lord, saying, 'O Lord God, remember me, I pray! Strengthen me, I pray, just this once, O God, that I may with one blow take vengeance on the Philistines for my two eyes.' Samson took hold of the middle pillars that supported the temple and braced himself against them, one on his right and the other on his left. Then Samson said, 'Let me die with the Philistines!' And he pushed with all his might, and the temple fell on the lords and all the people who were in it. So the dead that he killed at his death were more than he killed in his life."*
>
> **— *Judges 16:28-30 (NKJV)***

Samson was destroyed for lack of knowledge and self-deception. Sometimes, we become paranoid and powerless over confronting problems. Many refuse to admit and address challenges and instead fall victim to self-righteousness. You may relate to some of the commandments that cloud our judgment and rationality:

"I am a grown man or woman and know what I want. I got this. This is not my first rodeo. I am in control. This is my life, and it's my business," without the slightest idea and understanding that we are closer to death and destruction than we know. Samson was one of the strongest, most gifted judges in Israel, but his appetite for women became an impediment to fulfilling his life purpose.

Just like every child of God, we fall short of our ministry and mission in life as a result of our appetites and worldly preoccupation.

Ellen G. White wrote:

"Adam, in transgressing the word of Jehovah, had opened the door for Satan, who had planted his banner in the midst of the first family. He was to feel, indeed, that the wages of sin was death. Satan designed to gain Eden by deceiving our first parents, but in this, he was disappointed. Instead of securing Eden for himself, he now feared he would lose all he had claimed outside of Eden. His sagacity could trace the significance of these offerings, that they pointed man to a Redeemer, and, for the time being, were a typical atonement for the sin of fallen man, opening a door of hope to the race."

SAMUEL

"The Philistines, moving eastwards to conquer the Israelites' stronghold, defeated the tribal armies and even captured the Ark of the Lord itself. The temple at Shiloh was destroyed, the people were disarmed, and Israel became a vassal of Philistia.

Samuel, the prophet, saw this disaster was caused by the Israelites' disorganization. The obvious answer was to follow the pattern of the surrounding people and set up a united nation under a king."

— Levinger and Gersh

In continuation of the search to persevere in this journey and to bring to my readers and audience the truth and best reasons for this study:

"The AUDACITY OF JESUS; THE SON, THE LAMB, THE LION, THE MESSIAH, AND HIS MISSION."

I have discovered that every great character and personality God used to fulfill His promises to Abraham and his descendants were men and women from dysfunctional, redeemed, and reclaimed families and their failures. But through God's grace, which metamorphosed into faith, they triumphed into God's super heavyweights at the altar of servanthood and the tracehold of discipleship.

The Psalmists, in one of their favorite verses, wrote:

"The Lord upholds all who fall and lifts up all who are bowed down."

— Psalm 145:14 (KJV)

What the Psalmists are saying is that our God is a Father to the fatherless. He is the Comforter, Redeemer, and Advocate.

So, where are you on the spiral of life's roller coaster? At whatever point you find yourself, you are probably not alone. Many of us have fallen, and it took the help of God for our deliverance. Our faithful, redemptive testimonies and miracles set the stage for God's salvation ministry.

Pastor Gary Inrig recaptures the story of faith in Hebrews 11 and suggests that the Hall of Faith be retitled "God's Hall of Reclaimed Failures." He continued in his submission:

"There is scarcely an individual in that chapter **(Hebrews 11)** without a serious blemish in his or her life, but God is in the business of restoring failures... That is a great principle of God's grace."

We speak about God's compassionate love and mercy when we reflect on Psalm 145. King David was a man after God's heart, and his praises of thanksgiving remain forever.

Let's backtrack lest we exceed our posted speed limit. I know it's difficult, even with the help of cruise control.

Samuel's birth was a result of fervent prayer from the sorrowful and anguished soul of a barren mother named Hannah. Hannah prayed with a broken heart, pouring out her soul as she wept. She prayed:

> *"LORD ALL-POWERFUL, I am your servant, but I am so miserable! Please let me have a son. I will give him to You for as long as he lives, and his hair will never be cut."*

— *1 Samuel 1:11 (CEV)*

Yes, God honored Hannah's prayer and vow in agreement with the priest Eli. Hannah had vowed to give her child to the service of the Lord at the Tabernacle if God blessed her with a boy. When Samuel was weaned, Hannah and Elkanah took the boy to Eli, the priest at Shiloh. Hannah said to the priest Eli:

> *"Sir, do you remember me?" Hannah asked. "I am the woman who stood here several years ago praying to the Lord. I asked the Lord to give me this boy, and He has granted my request. Now I am giving him to the Lord, and he will belong to the Lord all his life."*

— *1 Samuel 1:26-28 (NLT)*

Samuel learned to become a priest after his dedication and through the altar sacrifices made by Eli, the priest. The story of Hannah and her son Samuel evokes the spirit of faith, patience, and waiting upon the Lord.

Many of us, through afflictions and miracles, have professed the ministry of reconciliation with God for those who are heartbroken and overwhelmed by natural and human circumstances. We may feel that the God we once trusted has abandoned us. But no, that is impossible because our God is Alpha and Omega, the Beginning and the End (Revelation 1:11, NKJV). Here are the words of exhortation and encouragement from the prophets in the Book of Lamentations:

> *"The Lord is good to those who wait for Him,*
>
> *To the soul who seeks Him.*
>
> *It is good that one should hope and wait quietly for the salvation of the Lord...*
>
> *Though He causes grief, yet He will show compassion according to the multitude of His mercies.*
>
> *For He does not afflict willingly, nor grieve the children of men."*
>
> **— *Lamentations 3:25-33 (NKJV)***

Samuel became a great prophet, priest, and the last judge. He transformed leadership in the land of Israel from military radicalism to kingship culture, as was common in the land of Canaan and other European and African countries, including Egypt and Ethiopia.

Samuel brought the Israelites back to God but failed to discipline his children to obey the law of God, much like the parallel story of Eli and his children. In his old age, Samuel appointed his two sons, Joel and Abijah, as judges, but their leadership was marked by corruption and nepotism.

"For we wrestle not against flesh and blood, but against principalities, against powers, against the rulers of the darkness of this world, against spiritual wickedness in high places."

— *Ephesians 6:12 (KJV)*

The forces Paul refers to here as "not flesh and blood" are not humans but demons and principalities (evil spirits) controlled by Satan and his co-hosts.

Could Eli and his family, and Saul, have been deceived by these principalities? Were their defeats due to a lack of godliness and disobedience to the will of God in their ministries?

Look at this passage, as Samuel wrote:

"But the children of Belial said, 'How shall this man save us?' And they despised him and brought him no presents."

— *1 Samuel 10:27*

Who were the children of Belial? They despised him and brought him no presents, meaning they rejected his coronation **(1 Samuel 10:27b)**.

In contrast, examine where the "tire meets the road," the revelation of John, and how Satan, from the beginning, has positioned himself and the dragon to dislodge the children of God and His elect. Here are the words of John:

> *"And I heard the voice which I had heard from heaven speaking again to me, and saying: 'Go, take the little scroll which lies open in the hands of the angel who is standing on the sea and on the land.' And I went away to the angel and asked him to give me the little scroll.*
>
> *He said to me: 'Take it and eat it; it will be bitter to your stomach, but it will be as sweet as honey to your mouth.' And I took the little scroll from the hand of the angel and ate it, and it was as sweet as honey to my mouth. But when I ate it, it was bitter to my stomach.*
>
> *And they said to me: 'You must prophesy again about many peoples, nations, languages, and kings.'"*
>
> **— *Revelation 10:8-11***

Look at the word "scroll" as it appeared twice, meaning it emphasizes importance. The angel did not force John to eat it; rather, John had to demand it. This points out the fact that the revelations of God are not forced upon His children; we must seek them.

William Barclay has broken this passage down, and here is his perspective:

This picture comes from the experience of Ezekiel, who was told to eat the scroll and to fill his stomach with it **(Ezekiel 3:1-3)**. In both pictures, the idea is the same. The messenger of God has to take God's message into his very life and being.

The sweetness of the scroll is a recurring thought in Scripture. To the psalmist, the judgments of God are sweeter than honey and honeycomb **(Psalm 19:10).**

"How sweet are your words to my taste, sweeter than honey to my mouth."

— Psalm 119:103

It may well be that behind these words lies a Jewish educational custom. When a Jewish child was learning the alphabet, it was written on a slate in a mixture of flour and honey. The child was told what the letters were and how they sounded. After the initial instruction, the teacher would point at a letter and ask: What is that, and how does it sound? If the child was able to answer correctly, the letter could be licked off the slate as a reward.

When the prophet and the psalmist speak about God's Words and judgments being sweeter than honey, it may well be that they were thinking of this custom. John adds another idea to this. To him, the scroll was sweet and bitter at the same time.

What he means is this: To a servant of God, a message from God may be both sweet and bitter. It is sweet because it is a great thing to be chosen as the messenger of God, but the message itself may be a foretelling of doom and, therefore, bitter. So, for John, it was an infinite privilege to be admitted to the secrets of heaven, but at the same time, it was bitter to have to forecast the time of terror, even if triumph lay at the end.

However, King Saul was a brave soldier and built a strong army of 3,000 gallant soldiers. His son, Jonathan, was very militant like his father. Jonathan fell in love with his father's captain, David. Jonathan went to war against the Philistines with a thousand soldiers and defeated them at Geba **(1 Samuel 13:3-4)**.

The Philistines were humiliated by Jonathan and his army. Therefore, they regrouped against Israel. This time, their number of soldiers outnumbered the Israelite army. Many of Saul's soldiers were deserting him.

Saul wanted to offer sacrifices to the Lord as the Law of Moses demanded, to appeal to God, as tradition requires in times of trouble and in times of plenty. These types of rituals were normally conducted by the priests. Samuel had commanded Saul to wait for seven days for his arrival at Gilgal.

Saul's army continued to dwindle while the Philistine army amassed momentum. Saul, in desperation, perhaps not trusting God and His prophet, who elevated him to the throne as king of Israel, disregarded the Law of Moses and the warnings of Samuel.

"The official copy of God's laws will be kept by the priests of the Levi tribe. So, as soon as anyone becomes king,

> *he must go to the priests and write out a copy of these laws while they watch. Each day, the king must read and obey these laws so that he will learn to worship the Lord with fear and trembling and not think that he is better than everyone else. If the king completely obeys the Lord's commands, he will rule Israel for many years."*

— *Deuteronomy 17:18-20 (CEV)*

King Saul, despite the warnings from Samuel and the Law of Moses, thought that Samuel was late to the appointment at Gilgal for the sacrifice. Saul's reckless abandonment led him to offer the sacrifice himself, knowing that it was against God's law **(1 Samuel 13:9-10).**

When Samuel met with Saul, he saw that the burnt offering had been performed by Saul. When Samuel asked Saul, "What have you done?" Saul replied:

> *"My soldiers were leaving in every direction, so I had to offer the sacrifice for God's help."*

— *1 Samuel 13:11-12 (CEV)*

Samuel told Saul:

> *"That was stupid! You didn't obey the Lord your God. If you had obeyed Him, someone from your family would always have been king of Israel, but no, you disobeyed,*

and so the Lord won't choose anyone else from your family to be king. In fact, He has already chosen the one He wants to be the next leader of His people."

— *1 Samuel 13:13-14 (CEV)*

King Saul continued to lead the children of Israel in battles with his son Jonathan. The anointing of David brought a new spirit to his army, and a new rule of engagement set in. David became a son-in-law to Saul, his musician, and an army captain.

But Saul became a troubled king as the Spirit of the Lord had left him. David single-handedly killed Goliath, the major general of the Philistines—comparable to the "Hitler" of the Canaan land (1020–922 BC). Saul became jealous of David, and Saul redirected his army's efforts to kill David, whom God had appointed to replace him as king.

Saul never recovered, as the Spirit of God departed from him. His earthly wisdom was not sufficient to sustain him and his family. The end of Saul's dynasty makes a good read, as Milo Connick summarized it:

"This period transmitted Philistia's iron age into Israel's golden age (c. 1020–922 BC). Saul resembled a judge more than he did a king. He failed to centralize the government, levy taxes, or conscript an army. With a band of volunteers, he fought Israel's wars. With charismatic

leadership, he exercised authority over his tribes. His was a transitional time between the collapse of the confederacy and the birth of the powerful monarchy. Caught between two radically different orders, his life was cast in dark shadows. The Spirit departed from him. Samuel (who represented the old order) rejected him. David (who personified the new order) threatened him through his rising popularity with the people. After losing the battle on Mt. Gilboa, Saul took his own life."

Milo Connick's summary of King Saul is a wonderful précis but seems politically undertoned, lacking the spiritual basis that is a major characteristic of King Saul's satire (rise and fall). Saul ruled Israel for a period of twelve years, and his monarchy ended when he died by his own sword at Gilboa, along with his three sons: Jonathan, Abinadab, and Malchishua.

In concluding the passage on King Saul, Rabbi Lee Levinger wrote:

"His reign closed when he died upon his own sword after the battle of Mount Gilboa, grief-stricken over the loss of the battle, the loss of thousands of Israelite men-at-arms, and the loss of his own three sons."

DAVID

"Furthermore, the Lord declares that He will make a house for you, a dynasty of kings! For when you die and are buried with your ancestors, I will raise up one of your descendants, your own offspring, and I will make his

kingdom strong. He is the one who will build a house—a temple—for my name. And I will secure his royal throne forever. I will be his father, and he will be my son. If he sins, I will correct and discipline him with the rod, like any father would do... And your throne will be secure forever."

— *2 Samuel 11:6-16 (NLT)*

The story of David is like a super-hydria passionate homogeneity to King Saul's family dysfunction. Though they are interwoven, their pseudo-pedia have different colors.

In fact, the meeting, love, and relationship between David and Saul was a defining moment—a climax of God's collateral audacity to fulfill the promise He made to Abraham at Hebron:

"I will give this land to you forever; I will give you more descendants than the specks of dust on the earth, and someday, it will be easier to count the specks of dust than to count your descendants."

— *Genesis 13:16 (CEV)*

What you discover in this metamorphosis is what happens to the "tire when it meets the road." David grew in obedience, humility, and strength as he attended to his father's sheep in the desert. As David continued to attend to his father's business, the Lord was with him.

Obedience to every master's assignment creates opportunities for glorious blessings, honor, and rewards. Obedience is not a gift from God; rather, obedience is a virtue to the gift of faith. By the victory of obedience, men like Gideon and his under-equipped army defeated the vast military might of the Midianites. God subdued the Midianites with His mighty power.

Paul fought in his ministry and mission with amazing faith, fueled by the knowledge of his passion to employ and expedite the mission of Jesus and the Good News message.

"I have died, but Christ lives in me. And I now live by faith in the Son of God, who loved me and gave His life for me."

— Galatians 2:20 (CEV)

God's generosity and desire to provide King David to the children of Israel was a way to show His love and promise to Abraham and his descendants. God provided David with everything he needed to succeed as a powerful king. God commanded Prophet Samuel to go to Bethlehem and anoint a man He had chosen to be king for the Israelites:

"Samuel, I have rejected Saul, and I refuse to let him be king any longer. Stop feeling sad about him. Put some oil in a small container and go visit a man called Jesse, who lives in Bethlehem. I have chosen one of his sons to be my king."

— 1 Samuel 16:1 (CEV)

Jesse had eight sons, and the oldest son was Eliab. Eliab was tall, handsome, and built with a kingly physique. However, when Eliab appeared to Samuel, his appearance nearly played a trick on Samuel. But the Lord reminded him not to be deceived by physical appearances and looks but to employ spiritual knowledge:

> *⁶ When Jesse and his sons arrived, Samuel noticed Jesse's oldest son, Eliab. 'He has to be the one the Lord has chosen,' Samuel said to himself.*
>
> *⁷ But the Lord told him, 'Samuel, don't think Eliab is the one just because he's tall and handsome. He isn't the one I've chosen. People judge others by what they look like, but I judge people by what is in their hearts.'"*
>
> **— *1 Samuel 16:6-7 (CEV)***

The second son, Abinadab, came to meet Samuel, but he was not chosen by the Lord. Shammah came to Samuel, but Samuel, disappointedly, announced that he wasn't the one either. All seven sons of Jesse appeared before Samuel, but none of them were chosen.

Surprisingly, Samuel asked Jesse, "Do you have any other sons? Because these seven have not found favor with God to become king."

> *"¹¹ 'Do you have any other sons?' 'Yes,' Jesse answered. 'My youngest son, David, is out taking care of the sheep.'*
>
> *"Send for him," Samuel said. "We won't start the ceremony until he gets here."*

> ¹² *Jesse sent for David. He was a healthy, good-looking boy with a sparkle in his eyes. As soon as David arrived, the Lord told Samuel, "He's the one. Get up and pour the olive oil on his head."*
>
> ¹³ *Samuel poured the oil on David's head while his brothers watched. At that moment, the Spirit of the Lord took control of David and stayed with him from then on.*

— *1 Samuel 16:11-13 (CEV)*

The anointing of King David became a defining moment in the life and history of the Israelites—the dawning of a shooting star, the landing of an eagle, a poet, a deal-maker, a visionary, a giant killer, and the grandfather of the Messiah, Jesus Christ. What a grand résumé! For one man, even our great God who chose David described him as a "man after His own heart."

But David was equally human, with a "jacked-up jacket"—a liar, a betrayer, a murderer, and an adulterer. However, it is not a surprise to note that every child born of Adam and Eve has different shades of colors; we are all born into sin.

David's affinity and love for God were completely opposite to King Saul's. He sought God's face and brought Israel back to God. The lost glory of God, which had departed from the temple due to the sins of Eli, the priest, and his children, was restored through Prophet Samuel's commission. His message was:

> *"If you return to the Lord with all your hearts, then put away the foreign gods... and prepare your hearts for the Lord, serve Him only, and He will deliver you."*

— *1 Samuel 7:3 (CEV)*

David's first assignment was to attack the Philistines, and he defeated them, reclaiming Jerusalem. His next plan was to restore the Ark of the Covenant to its former place in the temple. In his strategy, David consulted with the captains of thousands and hundreds and with every leader of the tribes of Israel **(1 Chronicles 13:1).**

In fact, King David, in his wisdom, could today be classified as a cum laude honor-roll graduate of his class. His mastery of diplomacy in leadership transcended his kingdom into a magnificent spectacle, more than any of his ancestors.

David respected the office of the prophets and took advantage of their messages and advice:

> *"One day, Samuel told the people of Israel, 'If you really want to turn back to the Lord, then prove it. Get rid of your foreign idols, including the ones of the goddess Astarte. Turn to the Lord with all your heart and worship only Him. Then He will rescue you from the Philistines.'"*

— *1 Samuel 7:3 (CEV)*

The children of Israel obeyed and got rid of their idol gods. Samuel became a part of King David's leadership, and through his guidance and prayer, the Israelites won all their battles with the Philistines, and the Amorites remained at peace with them.

David and King Saul's family had a love triangle saga. David loved King Saul and, unexpectedly, Jonathan and Michal. But King Saul hated David and hunted him, intent on killing him. God had told King Saul that he and his family had been rejected as kings of Israel, but Saul could never accept that as long as he lived.

The death of Saul ushered in the monarchy of King David, as Abner, Saul's commander, reached a secret agreement to hand over Saul's surviving army to David. David could not have married Michal, Saul's daughter, if Saul had lived.

However, Jonathan and David had a covenant relationship that even death could not break. David made sure to keep his promise to Jonathan's family.

At the death of King Saul, Jonathan, and his two brothers, David was heartbroken. He sang a song in memory of Saul and Jonathan, naming it "The Song of the Bow." David lamented their deaths as if they were his biological relatives. He directed that the song be taught to all the children of Judah and the use of the bow.

¹⁷ *And David lamented with this lamentation over Saul and over Jonathan, his son:*

¹⁸ *(Also, he bade them teach the children of Judah the use of the bow: behold, it is written in the book of Jasher.)*

¹⁹ *The beauty of Israel is slain upon thy high places: how are the mighty fallen!*

²⁰ *Tell it not in Gath, publish it not in the streets of Askelon; lest the daughters of the Philistines rejoice, lest the daughters of the uncircumcised triumph.*

²¹ *Ye mountains of Gilboa, let there be no dew, neither let there be rain, upon you, nor fields of offerings: for there, the shield of the mighty is vilely cast away, the shield of Saul, as though he had not been anointed with oil.*

²² *From the blood of the slain, from the fat of the mighty, the bow of Jonathan turned not back, and the sword of Saul returned not empty.*

²³ *Saul and Jonathan were lovely and pleasant in their lives, and in their death, they were not divided: they were swifter than eagles; they were stronger than lions.*

²⁴ *Ye daughters of Israel, weep over Saul, who clothed you in scarlet, with other delights, who put on ornaments of gold upon your apparel.*

²⁵ How are the mighty fallen in the midst of the battle! O Jonathan, thou wast slain in thine high places.

²⁶ I am distressed for thee, my brother Jonathan: very pleasant hast thou been unto me: thy love to me was wonderful, passing the love of women.

²⁷ How are the mighty fallen, and the weapons of war perished!

— *2 Samuel 1:17-27*

The divine order and plan of God will remain everlasting. Even from creation, disobedience—from Adam and Eve to the children of Israel, from Abraham to the present age—demonstrates that the wages of sin is death, and righteousness exalts a nation. Saul and his family learned this the hard way. The journey of life without God leads to destruction.

Charles Stanley (Dr.) wrote:

"Life is like an untraveled trail, with twists and turns. Appealing activities can become detours to the quicksand of sin. Engaging philosophies may start as small interests but turn into a mire of muddled thinking. Even the best route isn't always sun-dappled meadows and quiet riverside lanes. The only way to be sure we're walking correctly is to follow one who knows the way perfectly. God is the perfect full-service guide; no one can go wrong by keeping to the pathways He selects."

King Saul thought he was bigger than God. Even after God rejected him and his leadership, he refused to step down from the throne. He disengaged from Prophet Samuel and his divine orders, and the result was catastrophic.

There's a correlation between ignoring the Lord's guidance and ending up in trouble. The one who stumbles off course has trusted his own 'sense of direction,' his emotion, desires, or personal version of morality.

God's master plan to control and direct our lives is not in our hands. Many of us are afraid of failure, yet we wrestle with God in relinquishing power and control to our loving Almighty Jehovah Jireh.

Here's another perspective worthy of our examination:

"I know, Lord, that our lives are not our own. We are not able to plan our own course. So correct me, Lord, but please be gentle. Do not correct in anger, for I would die."

— *Jeremiah 10:23-24*

Prophet Jeremiah understands the pain caused by deceit and disobedience. His approach is one of submission and helplessness in admitting our sins and seeking remission and forgiveness from God.

In fact, King David was a class act in experiencing hopeless failures and crying out to God for His loving mercy and forgiveness:

¹ Help, O Lord, for the godly are fast disappearing!

The faithful have vanished from the earth!

² Neighbors lie to each other, speaking with flattering lips and deceitful hearts.

³ May the Lord cut off their flattering lips and silence their boastful tongues.

⁴ They say, "We will lie to our hearts' content. Our lips are our own—who can stop us?"

— *Psalm 12:1-4*

Now, let's reflect on David's epitaph for Saul and Jonathan, whom he loved:

"Our warriors have fallen in the heat of battle, and Jonathan lies dead on the hills of Gibeon.

Jonathan, I miss you most!

I loved you like a brother.

You were truly loyal to me, more faithful than a wife to her husband.

Our warriors have fallen, and their weapons are destroyed."

— *2 Samuel 1:25-27 (CEV)*

King David realized the power of God's agape love in his relationship with Saul and Jonathan. His soul bled when he heard that King Saul and his children were dead. David could have preferred to die if given the choice due to his unfailing love for Jonathan.

Remember, David had been appointed king by Almighty God, but Saul refused to yield the throne to David. Instead, he sought to find and eliminate David. Yet, when David had the opportunity to kill Saul, he refused to harm or destroy the anointed of the Almighty God.

Kenneth Copeland, a great minister of the 21st century, reacted to the power of God's love:

> *"To walk in love is to step aside and allow the power of the universe to come between you and the situation with which you are dealing."*

What an audacious revelation we grasp from Kenneth Copeland's reaction and David's lamentation in **2 Samuel 1:25:**

> *"How are the mighty fallen in the midst of the battle!*
>
> *O Jonathan, thou wast slain in thine high places."*

David stepped out of the way, went into hiding, and allowed King Saul to finish himself, strengthened by the fire and fury of God's love and His power. The power of God's love, when allowed to run its course, steps into the situation you are dealing with, as written in Scripture:

> *"Who shall separate us from the love of Christ?*
>
> *Shall tribulation, or distress, or persecution, or famine, or nakedness, or peril, or sword?*
>
> *As it is written: 'For Thy sake, we are killed all the day long; we are accounted as sheep for the slaughter.'*
>
> *Nay, in all these things, we are more than conquerors through Him that loves us."*
>
> **— *Romans 8:35-37 (NKJV)***

When you allow the spirit of God's love to step into your overwhelming situation and trials, Apostle Paul said we become more than conquerors. Hallelujah!

David never organized an army to fight Saul and force himself onto the throne that God had designated for him. David had the heart of a lion—after he single-handedly killed the strongest man in Philistine, Goliath—but he never allowed his warrior spirit to separate him from the love of God and the fear of His magnificent power.

David and Jonathan shared a committed and covenantal relationship, and their common faith in God's faithfulness was evident. Saul was jealous of their mutual understanding and their love for each other. However, their platonic relationship survived even Jonathan's death, and David took care of all of Jonathan's surviving family.

David could not have written a memorial song for King Saul and Jonathan if he had lacked the love of God and the unity of the spirit. How many in our millennium have similar spiritual qualities to David? Probably none. David was a man after God's own heart. His courage to forgive Saul and his family, and even to take Saul's daughter Michal back in marriage, showed David's Godly qualities at the beginning of his monarchy.

For every one of us, including those in authority, we should guard our tongues and hearts and avoid corrupt communication:

> *"And grieve not the Holy Spirit of God, whereby you're sealed unto the day of redemption.*
>
> *Let all bitterness, wrath, anger, clamor, and evil speaking be put away from you, with all malice:*
>
> *And be ye kind to one another, tenderhearted, forgiving one another, even as God for Christ's sake hath forgiven you."*

— *Ephesians 4:30-33 (NKJV)*

David's life should help us examine the way we love our friends and enemies. It is obvious that David succumbed to the spirit of adultery with Bathsheba and murdered Uriah, her husband. However, he honestly accepted his mistakes, took accountability, and accepted the consequences of those sins.

One of King David's greatest accomplishments was the return of the Ark of the Covenant to Jerusalem. But before the account of this dramatic and heroic return, let's address an interesting summary of King Saul and David's dynasties written by two Jewish authors:

> *"King Saul, following the teachings of the prophet Samuel, had put away those that divined by a ghost or a familiar spirit out of the land. But after Samuel's death, King Saul became frightened because he had displeased the Lord. So Saul went to see the witch of Endor before the battle at Mount Gilboa to see how the battle would go. In the battle, King Saul was destroyed.*
>
> *Even so, the divided tribe remained a united kingdom, made possible by Samuel's reinterpretation of the Law of Moses. A few years later, Samuel's successor, the prophet Nathan, thundered out against immorality in Jerusalem, even though it meant denouncing King David himself."*

— *Rabbi L. J. Levinger and H. Gersh*

Levinger and Gersh's summary of Prophet Samuel's warnings and cautions to King Saul and the children of Israel on the issue and consequences of idolatry, aligns with the advice and commands of Samuel to the kings and elders of Israel. Their account bears testimony to Prophet Isaiah's message:

"Come now, let's settle this," says the Lord.

"Though your sins are like scarlet, I will make them as white as snow.

Though they are red like crimson, I will make them as white as wool.

If you will only obey me, you will have plenty to eat.

But if you turn away and refuse to listen, you will be devoured by the sword of your enemies.

I, the Lord, have spoken."

— *Isaiah 1:18-20 (NLT)*

Both King Saul and David knew that "the wages of sin is death." That is a clear message in Scripture (as taught by Moses, Joshua, and Samuel).

What a great lesson for us to know God's truth. But here is the Good News: the blessings and gifts of Jesus Christ through God's grace and peace are available to us.

Apostle Paul, in one of his epistles to the Ephesians, wrote:

"Blessed be the God and Father of our Lord Jesus Christ, who hath blessed us with all spiritual blessings in heavenly places in Christ, according as He hath chosen us in Him before the foundation of the world, that we should be holy and without blame before Him in love:

Having predestined us unto the adoption of children by Jesus Christ to Himself, according to the good pleasure of His will."

— *Ephesians 1:3-5 (NKJV)*

The taste of the pudding, the icing on the cake, in this study and journey, are all invested in the person of Jesus Christ. He is the epitome of this great cathedral we are getting ready to build. So, relax and enjoy the ride as we uncover the book, *The Audacity of Jesus Christ*. It will not be easy; rather, it will take patience, faith, love, and hope.

King David returned the Ark of the Covenant to Jerusalem in a pandemonium spectacle. David was a warrior and a warlord. He was now the King of Israel, ruling from Hebron. All the mighty and small soldiers of Israel and Judah voluntarily came to Hebron to honor and support David and his kingdom. In fact, the celebration of David as king had never been witnessed in the land of Israel before. Everyone wanted David to be king.

> *"The soldiers stayed in Hebron for three days, eating and drinking what their relatives had prepared for them. Other Israelites from as far away as the territories of Issachar, Zebulun, and Naphtali brought cattle and sheep to slaughter for food. They also brought donkeys, camels, mules, and oxen that were loaded down with flour, dried figs, wine, and olive oil. Everyone in Israel was very happy."*
>
> **— *1 Chronicles 12:39-40 (CEV)***

These show a good testimony to prove that the hand of God was with David and his anointment as king. Obviously, David had leadership credentials in his DNA. After all, his great-grandfathers were Abraham, Isaac, Jacob, and Governor Joseph.

King David's IQ rating was beyond first class in diplomacy, as he exploited the advantage of democracy in his legislative procedures. He was a total contrast to his predecessors, Saul, Moses, and Aaron.

Therefore, David unequivocally would not rule Israel without God's guidance and Israel's acknowledgment:

> *"Then he addressed the entire assembly of Israel as follows: 'If you approve, and if it is the will of the Lord our God, let us send messages to all the Israelites throughout the land, including the priests and Levites in their towns and pasturelands. Let us invite them to come and join us. It is time to bring back the Ark of our God, for we neglected it during the reign of Saul.'"*

1 Chronicles 13:1-3 (NLT)

David exhibited the spirit of accountability, love for one another, and character in his leadership. This resulted in Israel's loyalty, progress, and popularity throughout the world.

The Philistines abandoned the Ark at the home of Abinadab. Abinadab had two sons, Uzzah and Ahio. David, his men, and a band of musicians were very excited that the glory of God was returning to Jerusalem.

> *"They went to Baalah of Judah (also called Kiriath-Jearim) to bring back the Ark of God, which bears the name of the Lord who is enthroned between the cherubim."*
>
> **— *1 Chronicles 13:6 (NLT)***

In the excitement and euphoria of the moment, David and his men committed the sin of sacrilege, which made God angry. Uzzah, who reached out to save the Ark as it was falling off the cart, was struck dead:

> *"Then the Lord's anger was aroused against Uzzah, and He struck him dead because he had laid his hands on the Ark. So Uzzah died there in the presence of God. David was angry because the Lord's anger had burst out against Uzzah."*
>
> **— *1 Chronicles 13:10-11 (NLT)***

The death of Uzzah sent shockwaves that disillusioned David's faithfulness in God. I feel the same way as David sometimes—our over-righteousness is worthless, a "filthy rag." But yet, David was a man after God's heart. He won an Oscar in the reviews of Almighty God. However, David was also human, an offspring of an earthly-spirited mother, Eve. What an identity crisis at the "cliff of family dysfunction mountain."

In life, every believer has the power of appeal in prayer. Yes, it is free and available with a contrite spirit. In case you forget, call 911—heaven—or go to your cell phone and log into Psalm 51:17. In case you're logged out, it says:

> *"The sacrifices of God are a broken spirit; a broken and contrite heart, O God, you will not despise."*
>
> **— *Psalm 51:17 (NKJV)***

God recognizes our helpless nature and our weakness, but "the wages of sin is death." In this life and journey to abundant life, our character counts and demands some level of discipline, which can only be achieved through righteousness and holiness, minding God's business.

As you read this book, and you have come this far, don't quit. There is a lesson, as I promised in the beginning chapters. This book will become a change agent in this world of crisis. Here are three-character illustrations you might want to share, written by Rod Hardley:

> *"After an immoral relationship was revealed, Gordon MacDonald said, 'I now realize I was lacking in mutual accountability through personal relationships. We need friendships where one man regularly looks another man in the eye and asks hard questions about our moral life, our lusts, our ambitions, our ego.'"*

Additionally, Jimmy Swaggart confessed:

> *"I fasted, and I prayed, and I begged God for deliverance from pornography. I realize now that if I had turned to my brothers in Christ for help, I would have been delivered."*

Chuck Swindoll stated:

> *"When I learned of someone's spiritual defection or moral fall, I ask: Was the person accountable to anyone on a regular basis? Without exception, hear me now; without a single exception, the answer has been the same: No! Howard Hendricks, a nationally known speaker and professor at Dallas Theological Seminary, studied 237 instances of Christian men who experienced moral failures, and he found only one common factor—not one of the 237 men had accountability relationships with other men. Those who are serious about living a pure and effective life before the Lord will find more strength when accompanied by true brothers."*

David knew he had a problem. As the first American astronauts lifted to the moon from Houston, "HOUSTON, WE HAVE A PROBLEM," everyone who came with excitement to bring the Ark home to Jerusalem was now fear-stricken.

David, down and hopeless, had only one question: How can I ever bring the Ark of God back into my care? David decided not to take the Ark back to the City of David, instead delivering it to the house of Obed-edom. He needed time to realign things with his Father in heaven.

Obed-edom was not afraid to house the Ark of God, but everybody else took to their heels. The Scripture reminds us:

> *The Ark of God remained there in Obed-edom's house for three months, and the Lord blessed the household of Obed-edom and everything he owned.*
>
> **— *1 Chronicles 13:14 (NLT)***

This proves that the Lord is a rewarder for those who trust Him.

As for King David, a man after God's heart, my guess is as good as yours—he learned his lessons. His meditations, songs, and prayers testified to his redemption:

> *"The Lord is my shepherd; I shall not want. He maketh me to lie down in green pastures; He leadeth me beside the still waters. He restoreth my soul; He leadeth me in the paths of righteousness for His name's sake. Yea, though I walk through the valley of the shadow of death, I will fear no evil: for Thou art with me; Thy rod and Thy staff, they comfort me."*
>
> **— *Psalm 23:1-4 (NKJV)***

The second paragraph of the song says, "He restoreth my soul." God restored David's hopelessness, grief, and anger. God is in the restoration business. Whether you have lost your direction, are down and hopeless in prison, living homeless, facing divorce, have lost your home, lost a loved one, or have been stricken with a terminal illness with no hope from the doctor—this is not the end of the road for you. Be still as you listen to the still voice: "I shall not leave you nor forsake you." This is the Word of God for you! You are redeemed in the name of the Lord Jesus. Your recovery is on the way!

King David recovered! You will recover! King David went out and conquered the Philistines, and you will go out to conquer your enemies in every direction by the power of Almighty God. You will sing the song of thanksgiving like David:

> *"When the Lord turned again the captivity of Zion, we were like them that dream. Then was our mouth filled with laughter, and our tongue with singing; then said they among the heathen, 'The Lord hath done great things for them.' The Lord hath done great things for us; whereof we are glad."*
>
> **— *Psalm 126:1-3 (NKJV)***

Now, King David was ready for the second time to bring the Ark back to Jerusalem. David invited the six Levites and two priests, Zadok and Abiathar, according to the order of God to Moses, on how to carry the Ark.

> *[12] He said to them, "You are the leaders of the clans in the Levi tribe. You and your relatives must first go through the ceremony to make yourselves clean and acceptable to the Lord. Then you may carry the sacred chest that belongs to the Lord God of Israel and bring it to the place I have prepared for it. [13] The first time we tried to bring the chest*

to Jerusalem, we didn't ask the Lord what he wanted us to do. He was angry with us because you Levites weren't there to carry the chest."

¹⁴ The priests and the Levites made themselves clean. They were now ready to carry the sacred chest

— *1 Chronicles 15:12-14 (CEV)*

In obedience, David returned the Ark to the City of David, where he built a place for the Ark of the Lord. King David was very happy to have successfully returned the Ark to Jerusalem.

David asked Asaph and his relatives (Levites) to sing this song of thanksgiving to the Lord:

> "Give thanks to the Lord and proclaim His greatness; let the whole world know what He has done.
>
> … Praise the Lord, the God of Israel, who lives from everlasting to everlasting!"
>
> And all the people shouted, "Amen," and praised the Lord.

— *1 Chronicles 16:8-36 (NLT)*

King David's love for God was perfected through his character, dedication, worship, and fellowship—like a fire that could not be quenched. God reciprocated David's love with all-abounding blessings to David and his family.

As David recovered and rediscovered God's unfailing love after the shock of Uzzah's death, God's love eradicated his fears and the effects of disappointment. Sometimes in life, we are bogged down by storms and demonic afflictions to the point that God's love and faithfulness are questioned. Stand still and allow God to express His amazing love, which is perfected in His words, promises, and glory:

> *"There is no fear in love, but perfected love casteth out fear because fear hath torment. He that feareth is not made perfect in love. We love Him because He first loved us."*

— 1 John 4:18 (KJV)

David's fears disappeared, and he overcame the challenges of bringing the Ark of the Covenant back to Jerusalem. David realized the power of loving God and loving others. The discovery of the mystery of God's love elevated his spiritual life to another level of anointing. David was not only the political leader of the Israelites.

King David transformed from a spiritual mediocre to a spiritual heavyweight—a man after God's heart, an extraordinary author. The last time I checked the Old Testament's *Who's Who*, David was listed as the author of the longest book in the Bible, *Psalms*.

The book of Psalms stands as the greatest sought-after book among all the books of the Bible. Psalms are quoted as poems, songs to praise God, expressions of sorrow, lessons for Bible classes, prayers, festival celebrations, and expressions of thanks for God's blessings and creation.

One of the most mentioned verses is quoted and referred to about six times in the New Testament: Psalms 118.

"The stone that the builders tossed aside has now become the most important stone."

— *Psalms 118:22 (NLT)*

Dear reader, are you still there? Hello! The point I am stressing here is that, like David, when you uncover the "mystery" of the "love of one another," your life will never remain the same again on earth.

God's love and agenda were David's first priority and prerogative, and nothing undermined his commitment and dedication. In fact, Apostle Paul's epistle to the Romans reflects the parallel character of David in the pursuit of God's love:

"Who shall separate us from the love of Christ? Shall tribulation, or distress, or persecution, or famine, or nakedness, or peril, or sword?

As it is written, for thy sake, we are killed all day long; we are accounted as sheep for the slaughter.

Nay, in all these things, we are more than conquerors through Him who loved us.

For I am persuaded that neither death, nor life, nor angels, nor principalities, nor powers, nor things to come, nor height, nor depth, nor any other creature, shall be able to separate us from the love of God, which is in Christ Jesus our Lord."

— *Romans 8:36-39 (KJV)*

Like David, with divine wisdom, understood the "Rule of Engagement" in his journey with God and the pursuit of the eternal kingdom. The Word of God is permanent and forever, from everlasting to everlasting.

Abraham's blessings and the promises of God remained with the children of Israel as long as they walked in the covenant of God and obeyed His commandments:

"And it shall come to pass, if thou shalt hearken diligently unto the voice of the Lord thy God, to observe and to do all His commandments which I command thee... the Lord shall cause thine enemies that rise up against thee to be smitten before thy face: they shall come out against thee one way, and flee before thee seven ways."

— *Deuteronomy 28:1-7 (NKJV)*

As a believer in the Lord God, you are an heir apparent to the throne of God and Abraham's inheritance. Do not allow the devil (Satan) and his co-hosts to rob you of your blessings due to ignorance. There is no affliction or adversity—whether divorce, sickness, addiction, pornography, sexual immorality, hatred, jealousy, abuse, unforgiveness, adultery, or idolatry—that can stop you from knowing the Lord and obeying Him. That is what life is all about.

Apostle Paul, at the end of his downfall, came to the awakening of the knowledge of God. He was persuaded in his transformed spirit as he wrote to the Philippians:

> *"But what things were gain to me, these I have counted loss for Christ. Yet indeed I also count all things lost for the excellence of the knowledge of Christ Jesus my Lord…"*

— Philippians 3:7-8 (NKJV)

Wow! What just happened in the last verse from Apostle Paul? I promised not to bring in *Jesus* until the "Grand Revelation" of the Baby in the manger. It's quite difficult to leave a cake with a child and expect the cake to remain the same when you return. Seeking your indulgence, remain calm with me, and hopefully, I will remain within the box.

King David was blessed all around after he brought the Ark of the Covenant back to Jerusalem. He built a palace, and Israel prospered. God promised eternal blessings to David. David's compassion for God led him to think of building a temple for God and a permanent altar for the Ark. The king's prophet, Nathan, was invited to the palace by David, and he said to Nathan:

> *"I dwell in a house of cedar, but the Ark of God dwelleth within curtains!"*

> *And Nathan said to the king, "Go, do all that is in thine heart, for the Lord is with you."*

And it came to pass that the word of the Lord came unto Nathan, saying,

"Go and tell my servant, David, thus saith the Lord, Shalt thou build me a house for me to dwell in? Whereas I have not dwelt in any house since the time that I brought out the children of Israel from Egypt, even to this day, but have walked in a tent and in a tabernacle.

... Also, the Lord telleth thee that He will make thee a house.

And when thy days be fulfilled, and thou shalt sleep with thy fathers, I will set up thy seed after thee, which shall proceed out of thy bowels, and I will establish his kingdom forever. I will be his father, and he shall be my son."

— *2 Samuel 7:2b-14a (KJV)*

Nathan, the prophet, went to David and explained the vision and the message of Almighty God. King David's request to build the temple was granted, but God rejected David as the builder. Instead, God promised David that one of his offspring would be anointed as king and would build the temple of God in Jerusalem! What a mixed answer and emotional message for David.

Let's pretend to be David—a great king with magnificent power and the anointed approval of Almighty God. You have the audacious authority to build a temple for God, but then God says no. Remember, David is human, too. What kind of emotional reaction would you exhibit? Would you feel rejected and disappointed? What if you were wearing David's shoes?

How many of us can relate to this situation? Many, including me. Think about how many times you've had an appointment with the doctor's office, a child's principal, a job interview, or a date, and they cancel on you. Those appointments turn into disappointments, don't they? And what happens to our emotions? Most of us feel bad and defeated. Maybe we even swear never to forgive or give a second chance if offered.

But King David, as enigmatic as any human being could be, enlivened his spirit and recalled his audio files of prayers. If King David were not in the spirit, bitterness might have overwhelmed him. He could have rested on one of his favorite psalms:

> *"The Lord is my shepherd, I shall not want. He maketh me to lie down in green pastures; He leadeth me beside the still waters. He restoreth my soul; He leadeth me in the paths of righteousness for His name's sake. Yea, though I walk through the valley of the shadow of death, I will fear no evil, for Thou art with me."*

— *Psalms 23:1-4*

Although many people, pastors, evangelists, and believers like me would have thought Psalms 23 should be the right prayer in such cases when we struggle and are challenged, David, in the spirit and fullness of God's glory, knew that the appropriate prayer was one of thanksgiving. We should learn from David as we mature in our spiritual walk. Here is David's prayer before the Lord God:

"Who am I, O LORD God, and what is my family, that You have brought me this far? And now, O God, in addition to everything else, You speak of giving Your servant a lasting dynasty! You speak as though I were someone very great, O LORD GOD!"

— *1 Chronicles 17:16-25 (NLT)*

King David's acceptance prayer of thanks to God remains a memorable one for all Christians and believers around the world. His humility and acceptance of his fate—that he was not going to be the one to fulfill his vision of a temple for God but that his son Solomon would—are admirable.

Yet, David's disappointment and emotions never turned into resentment toward God and His decisions. David was a man of war and was honored by Israel and all the surrounding countries around the land of Canaan and Judea.

David had divine wisdom and a calming spirit in the face of adversity and tribulation. Remember, at this time, the Holy Spirit, the third person of the Trinity, had not yet been given to man.

Earthly riches, wisdom, and military might were never a distraction to David's love for God. This becomes a constant reminder to the children of God not to take pride in their riches, status, or affluence. David understood and was conscious of God's warnings about boasting. Instead, men ought to glory in the words of Almighty Jehovah:

"Thus says the LORD, 'Let not the wise man glory in his wisdom. Let not the mighty man glory in his might. Nor let the rich man glory in his riches. But let him who glories glory in this, that he understands and knows Me, that I am the Lord, exercising loving kindness, judgment, and righteousness in the earth. For in these, I delight,' says the LORD."

— *Jeremiah 9:23-24 (NKJV)*

Prophet Jeremiah brings this Word of God home. If we are to boast and glory, it should be in the knowledge and understanding of knowing the Lord God as our all in all.

Many of God's followers today, worldwide, are ashamed of the gospel, while these same people boast and have virtual religions centered on their favorite sports teams and clubs. They idolize their superstars and are die-hard fans, so to speak! But when it comes to the gospel and the pursuit of God, they take a passive interest and display abysmal (wretched) ignorance.

Rod Handley wrote:

"David's life reminds us that integrity must continually be built in our lives through the disciplines of our faith in Jesus Christ. We cannot place confidence in our own integrity and relax and become lazy, or we will soon regress into a pitiful state."

Ted Engstrom said:

"No matter how much we try to hide our actions, our integrity (or lack of it) always shows through."

David climbed the pinnacle of power, authority, and influence—a pillar in Israel's "Hall of Fame" decorated with a "Purple Heart" among the Jewish people.

Yet, King David remained humble, compassionate, and hungry for the presence and relationship with God. The Almighty God responds and welcomes every pure and obedient heart. David won the admiration of our omnipotent God—a jewel of God's love personified, "a man after God's heart."

But unfortunately, David became complacent and vulnerable. He became a victim of his own lamentation: "How the mighty have fallen!" And the apple of God's eye became infested.

How could this happen to a man of God, wearing custom-designed apparel (a coat) of many colors? The answer is simple: David was human and lived in a sin-infested world. Perhaps he slept... bad news. Ellen G. White wrote:

"He had worked the ruin of our first parents and brought sin and death into the world and led to the ruin of multitudes of all ages, countries, and classes. By his power, he had controlled cities and nations until their sin provoked the wrath of God to destroy them by fire, water, earthquake, sword, famine, and pestilence."

Brethren, we cannot make excuses for David or for the rest of the sinful world, as we disobey God's commandments and fall short of His glory. Every one of us is held accountable and responsible. This is why we need to embrace the words of Apostle John in his epistle:

> *"Greater love has no one than this, that he lay down his life for his friends."*
>
> ## *— John 15:13 (NIV)*

David's lack of responsibility and accountability in a timely manner brought shame, agony, and frustration to his relationship with the just LORD God of justice and judgment. Perhaps David became paranoid and delusional, and he failed. He could no longer please God because of sin, and all his human efforts and self-righteousness, vested in the laws of Moses, were as filthy rags. He could no longer approach our holy God:

> *"But we are all as an unclean thing, and all our righteousnesses are as filthy rags, and we all do fade as a leaf, and our iniquities, like the wind, have taken us away."*
>
> ## *— Isaiah 64:6 (KJV)*

These sins overwhelmed King David: his adulterous relationship with Bathsheba, his lack of accountability for his dysfunctional family, and his disobedience in taking a census of the people. The killing of Uriah, Bathsheba's husband, derailed David's monarchy like a speeding train and brought a tsunami of consequences to his rule and influence.

"The hen (rooster) has crowed at midday!" shouts a popular African proverb. What an omen! In African culture, when the rooster crows at midday, it signifies danger—an alert to the community.

The death of King Saul and his son Jonathan grieved David, and he wrote the elegy as he sang, "How have the mighty fallen!" Regardless of the fact that David was Saul's enemy and nightmare, his love for Jonathan and for God was sufficient to sustain the moment for David and the entire Jewish community to mourn Saul and Jonathan during their rite of passage.

Tim Gustafson wrote:

"Even the best goodbyes are oh-so-difficult. But for those who trust in the LORD, the memory is much more sweet than bitter, for it is then we can honor those who have served others."

Oh, King David, cajoled by the spirit of Delilah at the threshold of adultery, murder, and disobedience—who will devote time to write an elegy for the people's king? "How the mighty have fallen" indeed.

"How have the mighty fallen, and the apples of God's eyes been infested and destroyed."

— *Oakey Chikere*

Many believers and non-believers alike struggle with the question: What led great men like King Saul, David, Hitler, Jezebel, heads of state, presidents, movie stars, sports stars, and apostles to fall at the pinnacle of their successes? Is it pride, lack of humility, spiritual immaturity, discipline, or direction?

However, the world has found a generalized answer to this question. We have muddled our answers by over-crediting Satan (sin) and spiritual warfare. Many of God's children are confused, seeking true meaning in life and wisdom to navigate the road to spiritual maturity and freedom from bondage. Here is a clip from spiritual transformation by John Ortberg:

> *"Pride is the oldest sin, and no matter what form it takes, it is rooted in our attempt to be like God. Pride has been a persistent problem for the human race since the Garden of Eden. It leads us to be preoccupied with ourselves and shun correction. It damages our relationships. At its deepest level, pride causes us to exclude God and other people from their rightful place in our hearts. Spiritual life is to love God and to love people. Pride destroys our capacity to love. No matter how well hidden it may be, we all struggle with pride."*

Ortberg draws our attention to the hard areas of our struggles. Do you feel you are always right? When was the last time you had a reality check on your relationships? Is any of your relationships on life support, waiting for a miracle to happen? Where are you sensitive to being corrupted? Are you willing and ready to accept responsibility for your failures and be accountable, even when criticized, regardless of the consequences? Have you always considered yourself more important than others?

God is calling you, me, and the entire world to take a moment and revisit King David's saga. What a tragedy! A mighty man of valor, an ambassador of our excellent God. My nerves are weak to write about King David's sins—more than the Bible and other prolific writers have already recorded.

We, as children of God, must consistently seek and pursue spiritual maturity in our walk with God and His kingdom. For more about David and Bathsheba, read 2 Samuel 11 and 12.

Spiritual maturity and discipline is a topic many Christians are ignorant about, but I will share some insights into this area as we continue. Be patient as we get to the topic before the end of this book.

David had ten wives, and among them were Michal, Saul's daughter; Ahinoam, from Jezreel; Maacah, the daughter of King Talmai of Geshur; and Haggith.

Solomon's wisdom benefited not only the people of Israel but the world in general. His literary works on wisdom (*Proverbs*, etc.) have transformed into the "bread of life" for a world that is perishing and in need of edifying words:

"Trust in the LORD with all your heart, and lean not on your own understanding. In all your ways, acknowledge Him, and He shall direct your paths. Do not be wise in your own eyes; fear the LORD and depart from evil."

— ***Proverbs 3:5-7 (KJV)***

King Solomon trusted in God and his kingdom, and all of Israel prospered. People from all over, including the Queen of Sheba from Africa, came to Jerusalem with their entourage to see for themselves:

"And when the queen of Sheba heard of the fame of Solomon concerning the name of the LORD, she came to test him with hard questions. She came to Jerusalem with a very great train, with camels that bore spices, very much gold, and precious stones. When she came to Solomon, she spoke with him about all that was in her heart. So Solomon answered all her questions; there was nothing so difficult for the king that he could not explain it to her.

When the queen of Sheba had seen all the wisdom of Solomon, the house that he had built, the food on his table, the seating of his servants, the service of his waiters and their apparel, his cupbearers, and his entryway by which he went up to the house of the LORD, there was no more spirit in her. Then she said to the king: 'It was a true report which I heard in my own land about your words and your wisdom.'"

— ***1 Kings 10:1-6 (NKJV)***

What a spectacle and magnificent splendor of God's wondrous glory in obedience to God's faithfulness. Amen.

Hello, beloved! This may seem deep, and you are probably perplexed. What you are reading is the truth, which may set you free from obscurity and enable you to attain spiritual maturity and kingdom prosperity.

Please stay with me as you continue to enjoy this book. Meditate upon this scripture and use it as often as you can as you progress in your journey toward abundance in divine wisdom:

> *"But as it is written: 'Eye has not seen, nor ear heard, nor have entered into the heart of man the things which God has prepared for those who love Him.'"*

1 Corinthians 2:9 (NKJV)

Seek the face of God and His spiritual wisdom, like Solomon did, because that is all you need. The wisdom of God will erase fears, disappointments, failures, unproductivity (poverty), spiritual dryness, inferiority complexes, depression, and confusion in life.

King Solomon broke all barriers because he understood the importance of God's wisdom. When you seek and trust God's divine wisdom, here is the promise of God as spoken by the prophet Isaiah:

"I, yes I, am the one who comforts you. So why are you afraid of mere humans, who wither like the grass and disappear?"

— ***Isaiah 51:12 (NLT)***

This is the true Word of God and the beginning of your recovery from the affliction that has paralyzed your dreams, visions, and prosperity in life. "Arise and shine," like Solomon, and overcome your circumstances, says the Spirit of the living God.

King Solomon was a successful king in the eyes of God and man. He was a builder and a deal-maker. However, this led him to mortgage his moral responsibilities to different kings, people, idols, and their daughters to seal many of his worldly agreements.

His marriage to seven hundred wives and three hundred concubines may have resulted in his popularity in the eyes of the world, but to God, it meant complete failure and disobedience. However, Solomon was human—not superhuman—he was fallible and vulnerable.

Unfortunately, Solomon succumbed to the qualms and capricious demands of his wives to embrace their foreign gods and deities. Israel was plunged into idolatry, which his father, David, and God had warned him about earlier during his coronation as king of Israel.

> *"But if ye turn away and forsake my statutes and my commandments, which I have set before you, and go and serve other gods and worship them; then will I pluck them up by the roots out of my land which I have given them, and this house, which I have sacrificed for my name, will I cast out of my sight and will make it to be a proverb and a byword among all nations."*

— *2 Chronicles 7:19-20 (KJV)*

Sometimes, I am very hesitant to pass judgment or curse God's elects. Many people may oppose my argument, but lifting a verse from King David will help explain my point of view:

> *"Hide me from the secret plots of the wicked, from the rebellion of the workers of iniquity, who sharpen their tongue like a sword and bend their bows to shoot their arrows—bitter words—that they may shoot in secret at the blameless."*

— *Psalms 64:2-4 (KJV)*

These were the words of David when attacked by Saul. David had the opportunity to kill Saul, but with insight into spiritual knowledge and understanding, he knew that God would oppose the killing and destruction of His anointed.

King Balak of Moab had asked Balaam to curse Israel, but God charged Balaam to bless Israel instead. Therefore, we must be careful how we employ our tongues in loose talk and worthless statements. Rather, it is a blessing to use our tongues to uplift and bless one another.

Note another statement from Balaam:

"How shall I curse whom God has not cursed? Or how shall I defy whom the LORD has not defied?"

— Numbers 23:8 (KJV)

The Almighty God is sovereign, and these words can never fail. He predestined Abraham and his descendants—the children of Israel (Jacob). We should always seek the face of God and His anointing power to be able to see and understand the words of God in the scripture and the teachings of His prophets:

"Oh, that they had such a heart in them, that they would fear me and always keep all my commandments, that it might be well with them and with their children forever!"

— Deuteronomy 5:29 (KJV)

God's Word to the children of Israel was a divine order—the law and the way things should be for them and later generations. The Lord proved this when His glory manifested on the mountain at the sacrifice of thanks for the gift of the law to Moses. Anytime the children of God obey and keep God's commands, He appears in His glory. We will see the next manifestation of His glory with the dedication of His temple by King Solomon in Jerusalem. Our God is happy when we obey, worship, and praise Him in His holiness.

When the temple of God was finished, King Solomon brought in everything his father had dedicated, including the silver, gold, and furnishings. They were placed in the treasuries of the house of God **(2 Chronicles 5:1)**.

King Solomon assembled all the elders, the leaders, priests, and the children of Israel. He brought in the musicians and the instrumentalists as they lifted up their voices in praise and thanksgiving:

"For He is good, for His mercy endures forever."

*— **2 Chronicles 5:13 (KJV)***

"So that the priests could not continue ministering because of the cloud; for the glory of the Lord filled the house of God."

*— **2 Chronicles 5:13-14 (KJV)***

Then Solomon spoke:

"The Lord said He would dwell in the dark cloud. I have surely built You an exalted house, a place for You to dwell in forever."

*— **2 Chronicles 6:1-2 (KJV)***

Solomon then spoke to the entire assembly and said:

"Blessed be the Lord God of Israel, who has fulfilled with His hands what He spoke with His mouth to my father David, saying, 'Since the day that I brought My people out of the land of Egypt, I have chosen no city from any tribe of Israel in which to build a house, that My name might be there, nor did I choose any man to be a ruler over My people Israel. Yet I have chosen Jerusalem, that My name may be there, and I have chosen David to be over My people Israel.'"

— *2 Chronicles 6:3-7 (KJV)*

Finally, King Solomon dedicated the temple with a prayer:

"Lord God of Israel, there is no other God in heaven or earth like You, who keeps Your covenant and mercy with Your servants who walk before You with all their hearts.

You have kept what You promised Your servant David, my father."

— *2 Chronicles 6:14-18 (KJV)*

When King Solomon completed his dedication prayer and sacrifices, something magnificent happened:

> *"The fire came down from heaven and consumed the burnt offering and the sacrifices, and the glory of the Lord filled the house. And the priests could not enter into the house of the Lord because the glory of the Lord had filled the Lord's house.*
>
> *And when the children of Israel saw how the fire came down and the glory of the Lord upon the house, they bowed themselves with their faces to the ground upon the pavement, and worshiped and praised God, saying, 'For He is good, for His mercy endures forever.'*
>
> *Then, the king and all the people offered sacrifices before the Lord. And King Solomon offered a sacrifice of twenty-two thousand oxen and one hundred and twenty thousand sheep. So the king and all the people dedicated the house of God."*

— *2 Chronicles 7:1-5 (KJV)*

King Solomon was happy for the mission accomplished to the glory of God. He kept the feast open for seven days, with all of Israel and the congregation:

> *"They kept the dedication of the altar for seven days and the feast for seven days."*

— *2 Chronicles 7:9b (KJV)*

We can all learn from the experience of Solomon that all assignments are possible with God. Here is an insight from Dr. Tony Evans on relying on God's faithfulness and thanksgiving:

"It is God who gives you the power to make wealth. I will humble myself underneath His mighty hand so that He may exalt me at the proper time. I will cast all my anxiety on Him because He cares for me. And when the chief shepherd appears, I will receive the unfading crown of glory."

Finally, in concluding this chapter on King Solomon, it is interesting to contrast with this brief by a Jewish writer:

"The third and last king of Israel was Solomon, son of David. His reign was a time of peace and growth. Solomon's alliances with the daughters of neighboring kings extended Israel's boundaries and power. His fleets brought horses from Arabia and gold from Ophir in Africa. Israel was opened to the world, and knowledge of the world came back to Israel. Israelites learned the arts and crafts of the Egyptians and Phoenicians of Tyre and Crete. Solomon built the temple on Mount Moriah according to David's orders. But upon Solomon's death, ninety years of unity and growth ended. The nation was divided."

The story of David and his son Solomon marks the onset of a defining moment in the history of the Israelites and the presence of the eagles in the land of the birds.

CHAPTER THREE
THE WAGES OF SIN

Both King Saul and David knew that the **"wages of sin is death"**—that is a clear message in the scripture (Moses, Joshua, and Samuel's instructions).

What a great lesson for us to know God's truth. But here is the good news: the blessings and gifts of Jesus Christ through God's grace and peace are available for us to receive. The Apostle Paul, in one of his epistles to the Ephesians, wrote:

> *"Blessed be the God and Father of our Lord Jesus Christ, who hath blessed us with all spiritual blessings in heavenly places in Christ, according as he hath chosen us in him before the foundation of the world, that we should be holy and without blame before him in love: having predestined us unto the adoption of children by Jesus Christ to himself, according to the good pleasure of his will."*

— *Ephesians 1:3-5 (NKJV)*

The taste of the pudding, the icing on the cake, in this study and journey are all invested in the person of Jesus Christ; he is the epitome of this great cathedral we are preparing to build. So, relax and enjoy the ride as we uncover the book, *The Audacity of Jesus Christ*. It will not be easy; rather, it will take patience, faith, love, and hope.

King David returns the Ark of the Covenant to Jerusalem in a pandemonium spectacle. David was a warrior and a warlord. He was now the king of Israel, ruling from Hebron. All the mighty and small soldiers of Israel and Judah voluntarily came to Hebron to honor and support David and his kingdom. In fact, the celebration of David as king had never been witnessed in the land of Israel before; everyone wanted David to be the king.

> *"The soldiers stayed in Hebron for three days, eating and drinking what their relatives had prepared for them. Other Israelites from as far away as the territories of Issachar, Zebulun, and Naphtali brought cattle and sheep to slaughter for food. They also brought donkeys, camels, mules, and oxen that were loaded down with flour, dried figs, wine, and olive oil. Everyone in Israel was very happy."*
>
> **— *1 Chronicles 12:39-40 (CEV)***

These were a good testimony to prove that the hand of God was with David and his anointment as king. Obviously,

David had leadership credentials in his DNA; after all, his great-grandfathers were Abraham, Isaac, Jacob, and Governor Joseph.

King David's IQ rating was beyond first-class in diplomacy, and he skillfully exploited the advantages of democracy in his legislative procedures. He was a total contrast to his predecessors, Saul, Moses, and Aaron.

Therefore, David unequivocally would not rule Israel without God's guidance and Israel's acknowledgment:

> *"Then he addressed the entire assembly of Israel as follows: If you approve and if it is the will of the Lord our God, let us send messages to all the Israelites throughout the land, including the priests and Levites in their towns and pasture lands. Let us invite them to come and join us. It is time to bring back the Ark of our God, for we neglected it during the reign of Saul."*

— 1 Chronicles 13:1-3 (NLT)

David exhibited a spirit of accountability, love of one another, and character in his leadership. This resulted in Israel's loyalty, progress, and popularity throughout the world.

The Philistines had abandoned the Ark at the home of Abinadab. Abinadab had two sons, Uzzah and Ahio. David, along with his men and band of musicians, was very excited that the glory of God was returning to Jerusalem.

> *"They went to Baalah of Judah (also called Kiriath-Jearim) to bring back the Ark of God, which bears the name of the Lord who is enthroned between the cherubim."*

— *1 Chronicles 13:6 (NLT)*

In the excitement and euphoria of the moment, David and his men committed the sin of sacrilege, which made God angry. Uzzah, who reached out to save the Ark as it was falling off the cart that carried it, was struck dead:

> *"Then the Lord's anger was aroused against Uzzah, and he struck him dead because he had laid his hands on the Ark. So Uzzah died there in the presence of God. David was angry because the Lord's anger had burst out against Uzzah."*

— *1 Chronicles 13:10-11 (NLT)*

The death of Uzzah sent shock waves that disillusioned David's faithfulness in God. I feel the same way as David; sometimes, our over-righteousness is worthless—a **"filthy rag"** (Isaiah 64:6). Yet, David is a man after God's own heart. He won acclaim in the reviews of Almighty God. Moreover, David is equally human, an offspring of earthly-spirited mother Eve. What an identity crisis, at the "cliff of the family dysfunctional mountain."

In life, every believer has the power to appeal to prayer; yes, it is free and available with a contrite spirit. In case you forget, call 911 to heaven, or go to your cell phone and log into:

> *"The sacrifices of God are a broken spirit; a broken and contrite heart, O God, thou will not despise."*
>
> ## *— Psalm 51:17 (NKJV)*

God recognizes our helpless nature and our weakness, but the **"wages of sin is death."** In this life and journey to abundant life, our character counts and demands a level of discipline, which can only be achieved through righteousness and holiness, minding God's business.

As you read this book and come this far, don't quit. There is a lesson, as I promised in the beginning chapters. This book will become a change agent in this world of crisis. Here are three character illustrations you may want to share, written by Rod Hardley.

> *"After an immoral relationship was revealed, Gordon MacDonald said, 'I now realize I was lacking in mutual accountability through personal relationships. We need friendships where one man regularly looks another man in the eye and asks hard questions about our moral life, our lusts, our ambitions, our ego.'"*

> *"Likewise, Jimmy Swaggart confessed, 'I fasted, and I prayed, and I begged God for deliverance from pornography. I realize now if I had turned to my brothers in Christ for help, I would have been delivered.'"*
>
> *"Chuck Swindoll stated, 'When I learned of someone's spiritual defection or moral fall... I ask, Was the person accountable to anyone on a regular basis? Without exception—hear me now—without a single exception, the answer has been the same: No! Howard Hendricks, a nationally known speaker and professor at Dallas Theological Seminary, studied 237 instances of Christian men who experienced moral failures, and he found only one common factor: not one of the 237 men had accountability relationships with other men. Those who are serious about living a pure and effective life before the Lord will find more strength when accompanied by true brothers.'"*

David knew he had a problem, just as the first American astronauts lifted to the moon from Houston: **"Houston, we have a problem."** Every one of his musicians and followers who had come with excitement to bring the Ark home to Jerusalem was now fear-stricken. David, down and hopeless, had but one question: "How can I ever bring the Ark of God back into my care?" David decided not to take the Ark back to the city of David; instead, he delivered it to the house of Obed-Edom to give himself time to realign with his Father in heaven.

Obed-Edom was not afraid to house the Ark of God, though everyone else fled. The scripture reminds us that, for the three months the Ark remained with Obed-Edom, the Lord blessed the household of Obed-Edom and everything he owned.

> *"The Lord blessed the household of Obed-Edom and everything he owned."*
>
> **— 1 Chronicles 13:14 (NLT)**

This proves that the Lord is a rewarder for those who trust him.

But for King David, a man after God's heart, my guess is as good as yours—he learned his lessons. His meditations, songs, and prayers testified to his redemption:

> *"The Lord is my shepherd, I shall not want. He maketh me to lie down in green pastures; he leadeth me beside the still waters; he restores my soul; he leadeth me in the paths of righteousness for his name's sake. Yea, though I walk through the valley of the shadow of death, I will fear no evil, for thou art with me; thy rod and thy staff, they comfort me."*
>
> **— Psalm 23:1-4 (NKJV)**

The second paragraph of the song, **"He restores my soul,"** shows that God restored David's hopelessness, grief, and anger. God is in the business of restoring, whether you have lost your direction, are down and hopeless in prison, homeless, dealing with a divorce, lost your home, mourned the loss of a loved one, or have been stricken with a terminal illness with no hope from the doctor. This is not the end of the road for you. Be still as you listen to the still voice:

"I shall not leave you nor forsake you."

This is the word of God for you! You are redeemed in the name of the Lord Jesus. Your recovery is on the way!

King David recovered! You will recover. King David went out and conquered the Philistines; you will go out to conquer your enemies in every direction by the power of Almighty God. You will sing a song of thanksgiving like David:

"When the Lord turned again the captivity of Zion, we were like them that dream. Then was our mouth filled with laughter and our tongue with singing; then said they among the heathen, 'The Lord has done great things for them.' The Lord had done great things for us, whereof we are glad."

— *Psalm 126:1-3 (NKJV)*

Now, King David was ready, the second time, to bring the Ark back to Jerusalem. David invited the six Levites and two priests, Zadok and Abiathar, according to God's order to Moses on how to carry the Ark.

¹² He said to them, "You are the leaders of the clans in the Levi tribe. You and your relatives must first go through the ceremony to make yourselves clean and acceptable to the L<small>ORD</small>. *Then you may carry the sacred chest that belongs to the* L<small>ORD</small> *God of Israel and bring it to the place I have prepared for it. ¹³ The first time we tried to bring the chest to Jerusalem, we didn't ask the* L<small>ORD</small> *what he wanted us to do. He was angry with us because you Levites weren't there to carry the chest."*

¹⁴ The priests and the Levites made themselves clean. They were now ready to carry the sacred chest ¹⁵ on poles that rested on their shoulders, just as the L<small>ORD</small> *had told Moses to do.*

— *1 Chronicles 15:12-15 (CEV)*

They made themselves clean and were now ready to carry the sacred chest on poles that rested on their shoulders, just as the Lord had told Moses to do.

David, in obedience, returned the Ark to the City of David, where he built a place for the Ark of the Lord. King David was very happy to have successfully returned the Ark to Jerusalem.

David asked Asaph and his relatives (Levites) to sing this song of thanksgiving to the Lord:

> *"Give thanks to the Lord and proclaim his greatness, let the whole world know what he has done... Praise the Lord, the God of Israel, who lives from everlasting to everlasting! And all the people shouted 'Amen!' and praised the Lord."*

— *1 Chronicles 16:8-36 (NLT)*

King David's love for God was perfected through his character, dedication, worship, and fellowship, like a fire that could not be quenched. God reciprocated David's love in his all-abounding blessings to David and his family.

As David recovered and rediscovered God's unfailing love after the shock of Uzzah's death, God's love eradicated his fears and the effects of disappointment. Sometimes in life, we are bogged down by storms and demonic afflictions to the point that God's love and faithfulness are questioned. Stand still and allow God to express his amazing love, which is perfected in his words, promises, and glory:

> *"There is no fear in love, but perfect love casteth out fear because fear hath torment. He that feareth is not made perfect in love. We love him because he first loved us."*

— *1 John 4:18 (NKJV)*

David's fears disappeared, and he overcame the challenges of bringing the Ark of the Covenant back to Jerusalem. David realized the power of loving God and loving others. The discovery of the mystery of God's love elevated David's spiritual life to another level of anointing. David was not only the political leader of the Israelites.

King David transformed and graduated from a spiritual mediocre to a spiritual heavyweight—a man after God's own heart, an extraordinary author. The last time I checked, in the Old Testament "Who's Who," David was credited as the author of the longest book in the Bible, *Psalms*.

The book of Psalms stands as the most sought-after among all the books of the Bible. The Psalms are quoted as poems, songs to praise God, expressions of sorrow, lessons for Bible classes, prayers, festival celebrations, and expressions of thanks to God for his blessings and creation. One of the most mentioned verses, quoted about six times in the New Testament, is Psalms 118:

> *"The stone that the builders tossed aside has now become the most important stone."*
>
> **— *Psalms 118:22 (NKJV)***

Dear reader, are you still there? Hello! The point I am stressing here is that, like David, when you uncover the mystery of the "love of one another," your life will never remain the same again on earth.

God's love and agenda were David's first priority and prerogative, and nothing undermined his commitment and dedication. In fact, the Apostle Paul's epistle to the Romans reflects a parallel to David's character in his pursuit of God's love:

> *"Who shall separate us from the love of Christ? Shall tribulation, or distress, or persecution, or famine, or nakedness, or peril, or sword?*
>
> *As it is written, 'For thy sake we are killed all day long; we are accounted as sheep for the slaughter.'*
>
> *Nay, in all these things, we are more than conquerors through him who loved us. For I am persuaded that neither death, nor life, nor angels, nor principalities, nor powers, nor things present, nor things to come, nor height, nor depth, nor any other creature, shall be able to separate us from the love of God, which is in Christ Jesus our Lord."*
>
> **— *Romans 8:36-39 (NKJV)***

Like David, with divine wisdom, he understood the "Rule of Engagement" in his journey with God and the pursuit of an eternal kingdom. The word of God is permanent and is forever, from everlasting to everlasting.

> *"And it shall come to pass, if thou shalt hearken diligently unto the voice of the Lord thy God, to observe and to do all his commandments which I command thee… the Lord*

shall cause thine enemies that rise up against thee to be smitten before thy face: they shall come out against thee one way, and flee before thee seven ways."

— *Deuteronomy 28:1-7 (NKJV)*

As a believer in the Lord God, you are an heir apparent to the throne of God and Abraham's inheritance. Do not allow the devil (Satan) and his cohorts to rob you of your blessings due to ignorance. There is no affliction or adversity, whether it be divorce, sickness, addiction, pornography, sexual immorality, hatred, jealousy, abuse, unforgiveness, adultery, or idolatry, that cannot be overcome by knowing and obeying God, which is what life is all about.

The Apostle Paul, at the end of his downfall, came to the awakening of the knowledge of God. He was persuaded in his transformed spirit as he wrote to the Philippians:

"But what things were gains to me, these I have counted loss for Christ. Yet indeed I also count all things loss for the excellence of the knowledge of Christ Jesus my…"

— *Philippians 3:7-8 (NKJV)*

Wow! What just happened in the last verse from the Apostle Paul? I promised not to bring in "Jesus" until the "Grand Revelation" of the baby in the manger. It's quite difficult to leave a cake with a child and expect the cake to remain the same when you return. So, seeking your indulgence, remain calm with me, and hopefully, I will stay within the box.

King David was blessed all around after he brought the Ark of the Covenant back to Jerusalem. He built a palace, and Israel prospered. God promised eternal blessings to David. David's compassion for God led him to the thought of a temple for God and a permanent altar for the Ark. The king's prophet, Nathan, was invited to the palace by David, and he said to Nathan:

> *Now it came to pass when the king was dwelling in his house, and the* L*ORD* *had given him rest from all his enemies all around,* ² *that the king said to Nathan the prophet, "See now, I dwell in a house of cedar, but the ark of God dwells inside tent curtains."*
>
> ³ *Then Nathan said to the king, "Go, do all that is in your heart, for the* L*ORD* *is with you."*
>
> ⁴ *But it happened that night that the word of the* L*ORD* *came to Nathan, saying,* ⁵ *"Go and tell My servant David, 'Thus says the* L*ORD*: *"Would you build a house for Me to dwell in?* ⁶ *For I have not dwelt in a house since the time that I brought the children of Israel up from Egypt, even to this day, but have moved about in a tent and in a tabernacle.* ⁷ *Wherever I have moved about with all the children of Israel, have I ever spoken a word to anyone from the tribes of Israel, whom I commanded to shepherd My people Israel, saying, 'Why have you not built Me a house of cedar?'"'* ⁸ *Now therefore, thus shall you say to My servant David, 'Thus says the* L*ORD* *of hosts: "I took you from the sheepfold, from following the sheep, to be ruler over My people, over Israel.* ⁹ *And I*

have been with you wherever you have gone, and have [a] *cut off all your enemies from before you and have made you a great name, like the name of the great men who are on the earth.* ¹⁰ *Moreover I will appoint a place for My people Israel, and will plant them, that they may dwell in a place of their own and move no more; nor shall the sons of wickedness oppress them anymore, as previously,* ¹¹ *since the time that I commanded judges to be over My people Israel, and have caused you to rest from all your enemies. Also, the* LORD [b] *tells you that He will make you a* [c] *house.*

¹² *"When your days are fulfilled, and you rest with your fathers, I will set up your seed after you, who will come from your body, and I will establish his kingdom.* ¹³ *He shall build a house for My name, and I will establish the throne of his kingdom forever.* ¹⁴ *I will be his Father, and he shall be My son. If he commits iniquity, I will chasten him with the rod of men and with the* [d] *blows of the sons of men.*

— *2 Samuel 7:1-14 (NKJV)*

Nathan, the prophet, went to David and explained the vision and the message of Almighty God. King David's request to build the temple was granted, but God rejected David as the builder. Instead, God promised David that one of his offspring would be anointed as king and would build the temple of God in Jerusalem! What a mixed answer and emotional message for David.

Let's pretend to be David—a great king with magnificent power, with the anointed approval of Almighty God, having audacious authority to build a temple for God. But God said no. Remember, David is equally human. What kind of emotional reaction would you exhibit? Rejection and disappointment? Imagine if you were wearing David's shoes.

How many of us can relate to this situation? Many, including me. Recall the times you had an appointment with a doctor's office, your child's principal's office, a job interview, or a date, and it was canceled. Those appointments turned into disappointments, didn't they? And what became of our emotions? Most of us felt bad and defeated. Maybe we swore never to forgive or give a second chance if it were offered to us.

But King David, as enigmatic a human being as he was, enlivened his spirit and recalled his "audio files" on prayers. If King David had not been in the spirit, bitterness would have overwhelmed him. He may have rested on one of his favorite psalms:

> *"The Lord is my shepherd, I shall not want. He maketh me to lie down in green pastures, he leadeth me beside the still waters. He restoreth my soul, he leadeth me in the paths of righteousness for his name's sake. Yea, though I walk through the valley of the shadow of death, I will fear no evil, for thou art with me."*
>
> **— *Psalms 23:1-4 (NKJV)***

Although many people, pastors, evangelists, and believers like me would have thought Psalms 23 should be the right prayer in most cases when we struggle and are challenged, David, in the spirit and fullness of God's glory, knew that the appropriate prayer was a prayer of thanksgiving. We should learn from David as we mature in our spiritual walk. Here is David's prayer before the Lord, God:

> *"Who am I, O Lord God, and what is my family, that you have brought me this far? And now, O God, in addition to everything else, you speak of giving your servant a lasting dynasty! You speak as though I were someone very great, O Lord God!"*

— *1 Chronicles 17:16-25 (NLT)*

King David's acceptance prayer of thanks to God remains memorable to all Christians and believers worldwide. His humility and acceptance of his fate—that he was not going to be the one to fulfill his vision of a temple for God but that his son Solomon would—shows his faith.

Yet David's disappointment and emotions never turned into resentment toward God and His decisions. David was a man of war, honored by Israel and all surrounding countries in Canaan and Judea.

David had divine wisdom and a calming spirit in the face of adversity and tribulation. Remember, at this time, the person of the Holy Spirit—the third person of the Trinity—had not yet been given to man.

Earthly riches, wisdom, and military might never distract David from his love for God. This is a constant reminder to God's children not to take pride in their riches, status, or affluence. David understood and was conscious of God's warnings, knowing that men should glory in the words of Almighty Jehovah:

> *"Thus says the Lord, let not the wise man glory in his wisdom, let not the mighty man glory in his might, nor let the rich man glory in his riches. But let him who glories glory in this, that he understands and knows me, that I am the Lord, exercising lovingkindness, judgment, and righteousness in the earth. For in these I delight, says the Lord."*

— *Jeremiah 9:23-24 (NKJV)*

Prophet Jeremiah brings this word of God home. If we are to boast and glory, it should be about the knowledge and understanding of knowing the Lord God as our all-in-all.

Many of God's followers today, worldwide, are ashamed of the gospel, while the same people glory and have virtual religion about their favorite sports teams and clubs. They idolize their superstars, becoming "die-hard fans," so to say! But when it comes to the gospel and pursuit of God, they take a passive interest and display abysmal ignorance.

Rod Handley wrote:

"David's life reminds us that integrity must continually be built in our lives through the disciplines of our faith in Jesus Christ. We cannot place confidence in our own integrity, relax, and become lazy, or we will soon regress into a pitiful state." Ted Engstrom said, "No matter how much we try to hide our actions, our integrity (or lack of it) always shows through."

David climbed to the pinnacle of power, authority, and honor—a pillar in Israel's "Hall of Fame," decorated with a "Purple Heart," a figure honored among the Jewish people.

Yet King David was humble, compassionate, and hungry for God's presence and a relationship with Him. The Almighty God responds to and welcomes every pure and obedient heart. David equally won the admiration of our omnipotent God—a jewel of God's love personified as "a man after God's heart" (1 Samuel 13:14).

Unfortunately, David became complacent and vulnerable, becoming a victim of his own lamentation: **"How the mighty have fallen!"**

And the apple of God's eye was infested.

How could this happen to a man of God, wearing custom-designed apparel (a coat) of many colors? The answer is simple: David was human and lived in a sin-infested world. Perhaps he slipped... Bad news. Ellen G. White wrote:

> *"He had worked the ruin of our first parents and brought sin and death into the world and led to the ruin of multitudes of all ages, countries, and classes. By his power, he had controlled cities and nations until their sin provoked the wrath of God to destroy them by fire, water, earthquake, sword, famine, and pestilence."*

Brethren, we cannot make excuses for David or for the rest of the sinful world as we disobey God's commandments and fall short of His glory. Each of us is held accountable and responsible. This is why we need to embrace the words of Apostle John in his epistle:

> *"Greater love has no one than this, that he lay down his life for his friends."*

— *John 15:13 (NKJV)*

David's lack of responsibility and accountability in a timely manner brought shame, agony, and frustration to his relationship with the just Lord God of justice and judgment. Perhaps David became paranoid, and he failed; he could no longer please God because of sin. All his human efforts and self-righteousness, vested in the laws of Moses, were as filthy rags; he could no longer approach our holy God:

"But we are all like an unclean thing, and all our righteousnesses are as filthy rags, and we all do fade as a leaf, and our iniquities, like the wind, have taken us away."

— *Isaiah 64:6 (KJV)*

These sins overwhelmed King David—his adulterous relationship with Bathsheba, his accountability for his dysfunctional family, and his disobediently taking a census of the people. The killing of Uriah, Bathsheba's husband, became a derailment of a speeding train and a tsunami to David's monarchy and globalism.

"The hen (rooster) has crowed at midday!" shouts a popular African proverb. What an omen! In African culture, when the rooster crows at midday, it signifies danger, an alert to the community.

The death of King Saul and his son Jonathan grieved David, and he wrote an elegy as he sang, **"How the mighty have fallen."** Regardless of the fact that David had been Saul's enemy and nightmare, his love for Jonathan and for God was sufficient to sustain the moment for David and the entire Jewish community to mourn Saul and observe the rites of passage.

Tim Gustafson wrote:

"Even the best goodbyes are oh-so-difficult. But for those who trust in the Lord, the memory is much more sweet than bitter, for it is when we can honor those who have served others."

Oh, King David, cajoled by the spirit of Delilah (Judges 1b) at the threshold of adultery, murder, and disobedience—who will devote themselves to writing an elegy for the people's king? **"How the mighty have fallen."** Here is one for our great king and friend:

> *"How are the mighty fallen and the apples of God's eyes infested and destroyed."*

— Oakey Chikere

The question a lot of us, believers and non-believers alike, struggle with is what led great men like King Saul, David, Hitler, Jezebel, heads of state, presidents, movie stars, sports stars, and apostles to fall at the pinnacle of their successes? Is it pride, lack of humility, lack of spiritual maturity, discipline, or lack of direction?

However, the world has found a generalized answer to this question. We have muddled up our answers by over-crediting Satan (sin) and spiritual warfare. Many of God's children are confused, seeking the true meaning of life and wisdom to navigate the road to spiritual maturity and freedom from bondage. Here is a perspective from John Ortberg on spiritual transformation:

> *"Pride is the oldest sin, and no matter what form it takes, it is rooted in our attempt to be like God. Pride has been a persistent problem for the human race since the Garden of Eden. It leads us to be preoccupied with ourselves and*

shun correction. It damages our relationships. At its deepest level, pride causes us to exclude God and other people from their rightful place in our hearts, whereas... spiritual life is to love God and to love people. Pride destroys our capacity to love. No matter how well hidden they may be, we all have some struggles with pride."

Ortberg is drawing our attention to hard areas in our struggles. Do you feel that you are always right? When was the last time you had a reality check on your relationships? Is any of your relationships on life support, waiting for a miracle to happen? Where are you sensitive to corruption? Are you willing and ready to accept responsibility for your failures and become accountable when you are criticized, regardless of the consequences? Have you always considered yourself more important than others?

God is calling you, me, and the entire world to take a moment and revisit King David's saga. What a tragedy! A mighty man of valor, an ambassador of our excellent God. My nerves are weak to write about King David's sins, more than the Bible and other prolific writers have already recorded.

We, the children of God, must consistently seek and pursue spiritual maturity in our walk with God and His kingdom. For more on David and Bathsheba, refer to 2 Samuel, chapters 11 and 12.

Spiritual maturity and discipline are topics many Christians are ignorant about. But I will share some insights in this area of maturity in spiritual battle. So, be patient as we get to this topic before the end of this book.

David had ten wives, and among them were Michal, Saul's daughter; Ahinoam, from Jezreel; Maacah, daughter of King Talmai of Geshur; and Haggith.

CHAPTER FOUR
THE LIFE, TRADITION, AND WOMEN IN THE GENEALOGY OF JESUS CHRIST

- TAMAR
- RAHAB
- RUTH
- BATHSHEBA
- MARY

In a historic Jewish community, the center of their social life is embedded in religion, which resulted in the creation of an amphitheater called the synagogue or temple:

> "The synagogue was the special province of the scribes who were its natural leaders. Priests rarely appeared there. When ten or more adult male Jews met for religious

instruction, a synagogue is born."

The Jewish tradition and lifestyle promote dependence on one another through a common homogeneous community. Most of their instructions and early education come from the Levites, priests, and scribes. The words "Levites," "priests," and "scribes" were traditional forms of addressing their teachers, but modern teachers prefer the word "rabbi":

[14] You shall bring his sons also and put coats on them, [15] and anoint them, as you anointed their father, that they may serve me as priests. And their anointing shall admit them to a perpetual priesthood throughout their generations."

— *Exodus 40:14-15*

The commission of priesthood belongs to Aaron, the brother of Moses (Levites). While of a lower class than the priests, the scribes were law specialists charged with the interpretation of the law of Moses. The law of Moses was a book of law and order that governed the people of Israel, and failing to keep and observe it brought adverse consequences to the people.

The synagogue served as a religious center for prayer, education, social meetings, and sometimes political activities. Hence, it reflects the life and social behavior of the Israelites. In the absence of the scribes, priests, and teachers at the synagogue, an elder was appointed to lead the audience.

Attendance at the synagogue is not mandatory, but the center is open daily to cater to the needs of the community. Some sections of the law are often read daily, and an interpreter with knowledge of the Aramaic language offers interpretations in Hebrew.

Attendance on Sabbath days, however, is mandatory by the law. The synagogue consists of the Ark of the Covenant and a 'Shema,' readings of Matthew 23:2, which represent some kind of creed or order of benedictions:

> *² "The scribes and the Pharisees sit on Moses' seat, ³ so do and observe whatever they tell you, but not the works they do. For they preach but do not practice. ⁴ They tie up heavy burdens, hard to bear, and lay them on people's shoulders, but they themselves are not willing to move them with their fingers.*

— *Matthew 23:2-4*

The history of the Jews or Hebrews in first-century Palestine is full of momentous hazards and fragmentations of culture and traditions. There have been generational displacements and diasporas as a result of famine, wars, slavery, and acts of God's direction in the search for freedom and the fulfillment of God's divine order for a place called home—the "Promised Land."

> *"The life of the Jews in first-century Palestine is a general term with similar hazards. Jewish life was not monolithic. It evidenced an astonishing variety and vitality."*

Through the hectic history of the Hebrews, different types of religious leadership arose: patriarchs, judges, kings, and prophets. By the first century of our era, patriarchs, judges, and prophets were no more, and kings no longer exercised religious authority. The Jews took their cues from priests, Levites, and scribes.

There were contrasts in their belief systems among the Pharisees, Sadducees, Essenes, Zealots, Herodians, and others. They held their life existence to either Hellenism or Romanism. Hellenism was the adoption of Greek cultism and tradition rooted in ancient Greece. Romanism characterized the affiliation with Roman political personal inclinations.

The Pharisees prophesied religious legalism. They were defenders of the law of Moses and pledged allegiance to piety. They would rather die than disobey the Ten Commandments of Moses, the law (Exodus). One of their outstanding characteristics was defending the law of the Sabbath:

"Remember the Sabbath day to keep it holy."

— *Exodus 20:8*

In today's ideology of political correctness, they would be considered progressive and legalists, but they were not part of the upper class. If you remember, our beloved brother Saul (Apostle Paul) was part of this group in Jerusalem.

The Pharisees became so adamant that, in 168 B.C., Antiochus Epiphanes tried to eliminate Judaism. The pious Jews refused to defend their religion because the case was fixed to hold on a Sabbath day. They supported temple worship and believed in all the books of the Old Testament. The book of Mark recorded some disagreements between Jesus and the Pharisees:

> *⁵ And the Pharisees and the scribes asked him, "Why do your disciples not walk according to the tradition of the elders, but eat with defiled hands?" ⁶ And he said to them, "Well did Isaiah prophesy of you hypocrites, as it is written,*
>
> *"'This people honors me with their lips, but their heart is far from me; ⁷ in vain do they worship me, teaching as doctrines the commandments of men.'*

— Mark 7:5-7

The Gospels contain many criticisms of the Pharisees' beliefs (Matthew 15:1-9). Jesus described the Pharisees as hypocrites. They tithed meticulously yet neglected justice with reckless abandon (Matthew 23:23-24). Jesus Christ was very disgusted with the Pharisees during His ministry. Sherman Johnson wrote his perspective about the Pharisees in Jewish tradition:

> *"There was no finer standard of righteousness in the ancient world than the Pharisees with its emphasis on personal holiness and social responsibilities."*

The reality, as Johnson wrote, is that the Pharisees enjoyed more influence than any other religious set, and yet, they were in the minority. They were social leaders who manipulated the common masses. Judaism in modern Jewish culture still stands as a major denominator in the political and religious equation of the people of Israel.

The Essenes were one of the minority groups within Palestine in Jewish history. However, there was another similar group known as the Zealots. The Essenes represented a spiritual sect that overindulged in Pharisaism. Their ancestors were pietists (a religion of self-piety). They lived in secluded communities or villages. Most of their characteristics are common with monks.

They upheld socialism, sharing private property and belongings as a common community—a kind of welfare distribution of assets and productivity. They believed in and practiced baptism by immersion (cleansing) into water, as the Torah recommended.

They were vegetarians, supported the temple but opposed animal sacrifices, and adopted a celibate lifestyle based on the belief that the world was close to its end.

The Dead Sea Scrolls are believed to be writings of the Essenes. These scrolls, discovered in 1947 at the caves of Khirbet Qumran, contained parts of the biblical scripture of Isaiah and portions of the Torah. Another scroll described the struggles of the "sons of light," thought by some to be the Essenes, against the "sons of darkness."

The Zealots were another minority set of the pious who declared war against the Romans. Their slogan was, "The sword and not sparingly; no King but the Lord." They were not recognized as a party until about 66 A.D. They were described as John's loyalists, the head of the Mayhem revolt against Rome (War iv, 3). Revolutionary groups emerged from Zealot origins, starting with Pompey's time.

The Sadducees were part of the Hellenist political party. They aligned themselves with Roman leadership, which helped them gain economic and political advantages. Their name seems to have originated from a branch of Zadok, Solomon's priest:

> *[35] The king put Benaiah, the son of Jehoiada, over the army in place of Joab, and the king put Zadok, the priest, in place of Abiathar.*
>
> **— 1 Kings 2:35**

Zadok, the priest, must have wielded significant influence on the spiritual roots of the Sadducees. Hence, the Sadducees invested great interest in administrative leadership and temple worship in Jewish history.

Here is Connick's perspective on the differences between Pharisees and Sadducees' political and spiritual inclinations during the Roman struggle:

> *"The Sadducees were friendly to Hellenism, and the Pharisees abhorred it. The Sadducees were wealthy aristocrats; the Pharisees generally belonged to the middle class. The Sadducees were conservative; the Pharisees were progressive. The Sadducees recognized only the Pentateuch*

as scripture. The Pharisees also accepted the prophets, the tradition of the elders, and later the writings. The Sadducees denied the resurrection, judgment, future life, angels, and spirits; all these the Pharisees affirmed. The Sadducees remained aloof from the people. The Pharisees canvassed... sea and land to make a single proselyte."

The Sadducees allowed their political and financial power to cloud their spiritual interests, losing their spiritual authority, which was rooted in Zadok's temple worship idealism. When the temple was destroyed in 70 A.D., the Sadducees disappeared, while the Pharisees persisted and helped develop new religious institutions in Babylonia. This contributed to the continuity of Judaism in modern Jewish history.

WOMEN OF AFFLUENCE IN THE GENEALOGY OF JESUS CHRIST

"He has cast down the mighty from their thrones and exalted the lowly. He has filled the hungry with good things, while the rich He has sent empty away."

— ***Mary's Magnificat***

The importance of women in religion and in the church cannot be overemphasized. In today's Christianity and its development, the place of women has generated substantial attention worldwide.

Hence, a rational conclusion in the study of the genealogy of Jesus Christ must include women of substance. In the documentary of the Gospel in the Bible, it is obvious that only Matthew included four women in the genealogy of Jesus. However, this study will address five women in the genealogy of Jesus Christ: Tamar, Rahab, the Mother of Solomon (Bathsheba), Ruth, and Mary, the mother of Jesus, the Son of God.

TAMAR

"I feel my path to heaven will be a long and painful one. I do not intend to work just for my own eternal salvation, closing my eyes to the people around me. No, I want to offer God many beautiful sacrifices so that I may help others avoid the pains of hell and reach Him in heaven. If my sufferings can help achieve that, what a joy!"

— Satoko Kitahara

The story of Tamar and Judah's dysfunctional family evokes sympathetic emotions and satiric euphoria in the corridor of desperation. There is a popular saying: "If the world gives you a lemon, you should make lemonade out of it." But in this story, it seems like Tamar got her lemonade and made super lemonade out of it.

Who could blame Tamar? She was human and lived in a world where no one wanted to lose out. To add to her injury, she was a woman born into a culture and tradition that marginalized the rights and privileges of feminine genders. Tamar was benighted with bereavement—death upon death of sweethearts. Probably, she got depressed, heartbroken, and zapped in overwhelming grief. Hence, she resolved not to drink from her teardrops anymore but to face her fears.

Tamar deduced an erotic plan to trap Judah, her father-in-law, in an adulterous encounter. Perhaps they might meet, and with hope, the encounter would result in a pregnancy and an heir to legitimize her marriage in Judah's family. This plan turned into double jeopardy in the historic story of Judah and Tamar.

Judah had three sons: the firstborn was Er, the second was Onan, and the third was called Shelah. Er, the first son, was married to Tamar. They had no child, but the wickedness of Er irritated God, and God allowed death to strike him. Tamar was left without a husband:

> *⁶ And Judah took a wife for Er, his firstborn, and her name was Tamar. ⁷ But Er, Judah's firstborn, was wicked in the sight of the LORD, and the LORD put him to death.*

— *Genesis 38:6-7*

Jewish law allowed a living brother to marry a dead brother's widow so that there would be an heir for the dead brother. So, Judah asked his son Onan to marry Tamar:

> *⁸ Then Judah said to Onan, "Go into your brother's wife and perform the duty of a brother-in-law to her, and raise up offspring for your brother."*

— *Genesis 38:8*

Onan, however, was not interested because he knew the child would not be his, as tradition demanded. Yet Onan had an obligation to his father and the law of the land, and refusal would have been very detrimental. Onan obeyed, but whenever he slept with Tamar, he ensured that his semen spilled on the ground to prevent her from conceiving.

> *⁹ But Onan knew that the offspring would not be his. So whenever he went into his brother's wife, he would waste the semen on the ground so as not to give offspring to his brother. ¹⁰ And what he did was wicked in the sight of the* Lord, *and he put him to death also.*

— *Genesis 38:9-10*

Sometimes, people in the world—including Christians—learn obedience in hard and painful ways.

Judah's youngest son, Shelah, was not yet old enough to marry Tamar. Meanwhile, Tamar could not raise a child by any other man outside Judah's family, or she would be stoned to death. She would either have to wait for Shelah to come of age or remain a widow. The law of the land demanded that a widow not marry outside the late husband's family:

> *⁵ "If brothers dwell together, and one of them dies and has no son, the wife of the dead man shall not be married outside the family to a stranger. Her husband's brother shall go into her and take her as his wife and perform the duty of a husband's brother to her. ⁶ And the first son whom she bears shall succeed to the name of his dead brother, that his name may not be blotted out of Israel. ⁷ And if the man does not wish to take his brother's wife, then his brother's wife shall go up to the gate to the elders and say, 'My husband's brother refuses to perpetuate his brother's name in Israel; he will not perform the duty of a husband's brother to me.' ⁸ Then the elders of his city shall call him and speak to him, and if he persists, saying, 'I do not wish to take her,' ⁹ then his brother's wife shall go up to him in the presence of the elders and pull his sandal off his foot and spit in his face. And she shall answer and say, 'So shall it be done to the man who does not build up his brother's house.' ¹⁰ And the name of his house shall be called in Israel, 'The house of him who had his sandal pulled off.'*

— *Deuteronomy 25:5-10*

Thus, both traditionally and spiritually, disobeying the law carries consequences. The story of Judah and Tamar portrays an entanglement of social and spiritual obligations. It is evident that the law of Moses could neither save nor redeem mankind. However, the Israelites needed law and order to sustain their daily living before the arrival of their promised Messiah.

Judah, being human, may not have recognized the underlying causes of his sons' deaths or suspected any ominous circumstances surrounding Tamar. Yet Judah developed a cold spirit and became fearful of Tamar.

Tamar, however, was not about to give up. She waited patiently and observed Judah's weaknesses. At the opportune moment, Tamar executed her plan, disguising herself as a prostitute. Judah, unaware of her true identity, had intercourse with her, and Tamar conceived twin boys—Pharez and Zarah:

> *²⁷ When the time of her labor came, there were twins in her womb. ²⁸ And when she was in labor, one put out a hand, and the midwife took and tied a scarlet thread on his hand, saying, "This one came out first." ²⁹ But as he drew back his hand, behold, his brother came out. And she said, "What a breach you have made for yourself!" Therefore, his name was called Perez. ³⁰ Afterward, his brother came out with the scarlet thread on his hand, and his name was called Zerah.*

— *Genesis 38:27-30*

Tamar, along with her sons Pharez and Zarah, became part of Jesus's genealogy as recorded in the Gospel of Matthew:

> *"Judah, the father of Perez and Zerah, whose mother was Tamar..."*

— *Matthew 1:3*

RAHAB

"Make haste to virtue in veritable love and take care that God be honored by you and by all those whom you can help with efforts, with self-sacrifice, with counsel, and with all that you can do unremittingly."

— Hadewijch of Brabant

The story of Rahab is one of covenant love, compassion, and trust. It invokes the spirit of transformation, challenging pride and subjective emotions that create artificial barriers. These boundaries often lead to a sense of superiority and a lack of humility.

John Ortberg addresses the issue of servanthood:

"Humility gives us the freedom to stop trying or pretending to be what we're not. It allows us to accept our 'appropriate smallness' so we can cease being preoccupied with ourselves and instead focus on and serve other people as Jesus would if He were in our place."

Rahab, despite her profession, was neither overcome by pride nor her environment. She was a harlot of professional acclaim, well-known even to the king of Jericho. Positioned strategically at the entrance of the city, Rahab commanded respect in her community.

Yet, when faced with the opportunity, Rahab chose to aid the Hebrew spies, recognizing the God of Israel as the true God. Her actions of faith and sacrifice ultimately secured her place in the genealogy of Jesus.

Rahab was, equally, a gentile prostitute, and her business targeted foreigners and visitors as her major clientele. So, here was an opportunity to make money and gain exposure. She could have exploited the opportunity by turning the spies over to the king, thereby elevating her status to that of a hero and a superwoman in Jericho.

However, something bigger than Rahab seems to have taken place inside her. Her spirit had been transformed based on the stories of fear and terror that had bewildered her people and the city of Jericho. So, immediately, Rahab saw the spies as they entered her brothel (inn). Instead of displaying her lowly character, "the Spirit of God took over her, and she started prophesying:"

> *[8] Before the men lay down, she came up to them on the roof [9] and said to the men, "I know that the LORD has given you the land and that the fear of you has fallen upon us, and that all the inhabitants of the land melt away before you. [10] For we have heard how the LORD dried up the water of the Red Sea before you when you came out of Egypt, and what you did to the two kings of the Amorites who were beyond the Jordan, to Sihon and Og, whom you devoted to destruction. [11] And as soon as we heard it, our hearts melted, and there was no spirit left*

in any man because of you, for the LORD *your God, he is God in the heavens above and on the earth beneath.*

— *Joshua 2:8-11*

Rahab's discernment about the spies recalls to memory the encounter between Lot and the two angels:

¹ The two angels came to Sodom in the evening, and Lot was sitting at the gate of Sodom. When Lot saw them, he rose to meet them and bowed himself with his face to the earth ² and said, "My lords, please turn aside to your servant's house and spend the night and wash your feet. Then you may rise up early and go on your way." They said, "No, we will spend the night in the town square."

— *Genesis 19:1-2*

The amazing question is: how did Rahab and Lot know these visitors were on missions for God? Divine connection or discernment? Your answer is as good as mine.

"Give thanks to the Lord, for He is good; His mercy (love) endures forever."

— *1 Chronicles 16:34*

"Faith comes by hearing, and hearing by the word of God."

— *Romans 10:17*

The word of God resonated in Rahab's spirit, and it triggered transformation. God's love is good and perfect, and

His love, compassion, and mercy endure forever. Rahab heard the word of God in faith. The miracles—the drying up of the Red Sea and the destruction of the Amorites and their kings, Sihon and Og—filled her with awe. Her passion for the children of Israel, their God, and the rescue of her household became her priority.

However, Rahab hid the spies on her roof in exchange for a covenanted promise: to spare her household when Jericho was attacked and destroyed. Here are the words of promise from the spies to Rahab:

> *"Our lives for your lives!" the men assured her. "If you don't tell what we are doing, we will treat you kindly and faithfully when the Lord gives us the land."*

—*Joshua 2:14*

Every time I reflect on virtues like compassionate love, humility, and sacrifice, my heart blossoms like a rose in God's unfailing love and faithfulness.

RUTH

"Jesus made no attempt to silence the Samaritan woman or Martha or Mary Magdalene, who addressed Him on theological matters. Nor would He allow His disciples to criticize the women who anointed Him with precious oil. Margaret went on to recall the faithful women who accompanied Christ on the way to the cross. "Thus, we see that Jesus owned the love and grace that

appeared in women, and by what is received as much love, kindness, compassion, and tender dealing toward Him from women as He did from any other, both in His lifetime and also after they had exercised their cruelty upon Him."

— *Margaret Fell*

The story of Ruth runs parallel to that of Margaret Fell, a prolific wife and mother of nine children. Margaret's life experiences, love, commitment, and beliefs became defining moments in addressing gender inequality in her religion and community in 1664.

Margaret married a wealthy judge, Thomas Fell, who was well advanced in age. Together, they pioneered the Quaker movement. In 1662, the Quaker movement faced imprisonment and disbandment due to anti-Quaker laws. The lives of this daughter of a wealthy Lancashire family and her affluent judge husband took a downward spiral into imprisonment, from which they never recovered. However, Margaret's faith and commitment to love never wavered.

In contrast, the story of Ruth—a Moabite in Canaan—unfolds as a meritorious drama, taking her from the pits to the palace. Ruth's story stands as a testament to love, faith, and resilience:

[16] But Ruth said, "Do not urge me to leave you or to return from following you. For where you go, I will go, and where you lodge, I will lodge. Your people shall be my people, and your God my God. [17] Where you die, I will

die, and there will I be buried. May the LORD *do so to me and more also if anything but death parts me from you."*

— ***Ruth 1:16-17***

The relationship between Ruth and Naomi continues to inspire. Ruth's love, faith, and commitment raise numerous questions for readers to ponder:

- Do you love your mother to the point of vowing to die with her?

- Would you die with your spouse to prove your love?

- Would you vow to die with your mother-in-law, especially after losing your husband?

- Would you worship the God of your mother-in-law if He is the true God, even if He differs from your own beliefs?

- If your husband passed away and you had no children, would you remain with your mother-in-law despite her reflections?

If you answered "yes" to two or more of these questions, then you embody the spirit of Ruth in our generation. My prayer is that God will crown your unconditional love. Amen.

Today, the world has watered down the word "love" to reckless abandon, attaching it to material things:

- "I love my house."

- "I love my car."
- "I love those shoes."
- "I love my school."

These material possessions are merely cosmetics to embellish selfish ego and pride. While materialism itself is not inherently wrong, it should never be mistaken for true love and affection.

The true love of Agape can only come through the Spirit of God. Ruth's love, faith, and commitment to her mother-in-law were pure, unselfish, and without material gain. This is the love God demands from us:

> "Whoever does not love does not know God because God is love."

— 1 John 4:8

Ruth discovered God's love in her heart for Naomi and pursued it with unwavering commitment. God rewarded her faithfulness, restoring all she had lost. The Apostle Paul offers timeless wisdom on love:

> [1] *If I speak in the tongues of men and of angels but have not love, I am a noisy gong or a clanging cymbal.* [2] *And if I have prophetic powers, and understand all mysteries and all knowledge, and if I have all faith, so as to remove*

mountains, but have not love, I am nothing. ³ *If I give away all I have, and if I deliver up my body to be burned but have not love, I gain nothing.*

⁴ *Love is patient and kind; love does not envy or boast; it is not arrogant* ⁵ *or rude. It does not insist on its own way; it is not irritable or resentful;* ⁶ *it does not rejoice at wrongdoing, but rejoices with the truth.* ⁷ *Love bears all things, believes all things, hopes all things, endures all things.*

⁸ *Love never ends. As for prophecies, they will pass away; as for tongues, they will cease; as for knowledge, it will pass away.*

— *1 Corinthians 13:1-8*

Naomi and her husband, Elimelek, along with their two sons, Mahlon and Kilion, left Bethlehem for Moab due to severe famine. The Moabites were idol worshipers, while Elimelek and his family worshipped the God of Israel.

During this time in the diaspora, Elimelek died, and Naomi became a widow. Now, Naomi was faced with the struggle of raising two boys and surviving hardship in a foreign land as a widow. I wonder how many of us can relate to her circumstances—her agony, loneliness, and the absence of close friends and family.

As for her sons, they were teenagers facing the challenges of adolescence. Boys will always be boys. Before long, they began to adopt the lifestyle of the Moabites. This was in stark contrast to their mother's plans and traditions. Hebrew adults were encouraged to marry within their tribe, but Mahlon and his brother, Kilion, decided to marry Moabite women—Ruth and Orpah. One can only imagine the kind of frustration and social pressure Naomi endured.

Perhaps God saw her plight and blessed her with affectionate daughters-in-law. Yet, the more Naomi struggled to climb out of the pit of hopelessness and grief, the more her condition worsened. As Colleen L. Reece wrote:

> *"Ten years later, Mahlon and Chilion also died. Naomi was rocked with grief. Why had Jehovah taken first her husband, then her sons? Now, only the two daughters-in-law remained. What should she do? Word had come that the Lord had visited His people in the land of Judah and ended the famine. Her heart yearned within her. Oh! To return to her own country."*

Naomi's last resolve and consolation were to return to her family in Judah, where she could be comforted by friends and relatives.

Before Naomi's departure, however, she was faced with one more difficult decision. She had to decide whether to allow her two daughters-in-law to return to Judah with her. Jewish tradition allowed widows to marry their husband's surviving brothers or relatives in what is known as levirate marriage. This type of marriage was not only common to the Hebrews but also prevalent in some tribal cultures and traditions in Africa.

Naomi had reached the end of her road, just as many of us do today. Life's afflictions had handcuffed her, leading her to a place of hopelessness. This reminds us of the words and vision of the prophet Amos:

> *"The days are coming," declares the Sovereign Lord, "when I will send a famine through the land—not a famine of food or a thirst for water, but a famine of hearing the words of the Lord."*

— *Amos 8:11*

The story of Naomi and Ruth presents a microcosm of worldly affliction and adversity, which seem to besiege humanity and demand immediate attention. Verses 12 and 13 of Amos chapter 8 help us understand that the famine Amos refers to is not physical food but rather the word of God and a relationship with Him—the spiritual food.

Naomi, Elimelek, and their sons may have lost focus and intimacy with their first love, the God of Israel, as they sojourned with the uncircumcised Gentiles in Moab. The word of God is clear and simple, as written by the prophet Amos:

> *[12] People will stagger from sea to sea and wander from north to east, searching for the word of the Lord, but they will not find it.*
>
> *[13] In that day, the lovely young women and strong young men will faint because of thirst.*

— *Amos 8:12-13*

This is a significant lesson in our journey of spiritual transformation. To withstand the audacious attacks of demons upon the children of God, we must understand that our present suffering cannot compare with the glory that will be revealed to us. As Apostle Paul affirmed in his epistle to the Romans:

> *"And those He predestined, He also called; those He called, He also justified; those He justified, He also glorified. What, then, shall we say in response to these things? If God is for us, who can be against us?"*

— Romans 8:30-31

Naomi gathered her strength, knowing that the journey back to Judah would be long. Yet, her love for her two daughters-in-law overwhelmed her conscience and judgment. She was ready to release them back to their families, where they could find new husbands.

However, how to break the news remained a mystery. The love triangle between Orpah, Ruth, and Naomi had deepened into interdependence. Obviously, neither eloping nor eluding was an option. Naomi had to face the music and reveal the truth. With a heavy heart, she prepared for a momentous separation. Her final words to Ruth and Orpah were filled with love and sorrow:

> *⁸ But Naomi said to her two daughters-in-law, "Go, return each of you to her mother's house. May the LORD deal kindly with you as you have dealt with the dead and with me. ⁹ The LORD grant that you may find rest, each of you in the house of her husband!" Then she kissed*

them, and they lifted up their voices and wept. ¹⁰ *And they said to her, "No, we will return with you to your people."* ¹¹ *But Naomi said, "Turn back, my daughters; why will you go with me? Have I yet sons in my womb that they may become your husbands?* ¹² *Turn back, my daughters; go your way, for I am too old to have a husband. If I should say I have hope, even if I should have a husband this night and should bear sons,* ¹³ *would you, therefore, wait till they were grown? Would you, therefore, refrain from marrying? No, my daughters, for it is exceedingly bitter to me for your sake that the hand of the* LORD *has gone out against me."* ¹⁴ *Then they lifted up their voices and wept again. And Orpah kissed her mother-in-law, but Ruth clung to her.*

— *Ruth 1:8-14*

This was a devastating moment for Ruth, Orpah, and Naomi, yet it was also a defining moment for Ruth. For her, it was the beginning of a new dawn and a discovery that would lead to transformation, abundant life, and the eternal Kingdom.

Orpah, unable to foresee the future, returned to her parents. Ruth, however, clung to her mother-in-law, refusing to take no for an answer. With steadfast determination, she pleaded:

¹⁶ *But Ruth said, "Do not urge me to leave you or to return from following you. For where you go, I will go, and where you lodge, I will lodge. Your people shall be my people, and your God my God.* ¹⁷ *Where you die, I will*

> *die, and there will I be buried. May the LORD do so to me and more also if anything but death parts me from you." ¹⁸ And when Naomi saw that she was determined to go with her, she said no more. ¹⁹ So the two of them went on until they came to Bethlehem. And when they came to Bethlehem, the whole town was stirred because of them. And the woman said, "Is this Naomi?" ²⁰ She said to them, "Do not call me Naomi; call me Mara, for the Almighty has dealt very bitterly with me. ²¹ I went away full, and the LORD has brought me back empty. Why call me Naomi when the LORD has testified against me and the Almighty has brought calamity upon me?"*
>
> **— *Ruth 1:16-21***

Naomi was knocked down and out as the enemy, King Devil, brought the fight to her family. She was down and refused to get up. She returned to Bethlehem, promoting her "pity party" instead of addressing her problems by seeking the face of the Lord. Naomi, like many of God's children, was overwhelmed by her problems. She was so blinded that she could not see the door of opportunity—Ruth—within her circumstances.

As you hold this book in your hands, can you identify with Naomi's challenges in your own life? I pray that this is the solution you have been waiting for to help you heal and "ARISE AND SHINE." Please, listen to me: in every affliction lies a great door of opportunity to soar like an eagle. Repeat after me: *Amen!* Meditate on and review this verse:

²⁰ And though the Lord give you the bread of adversity and the water of affliction, yet your Teacher will not hide himself anymore, but your eyes shall see your Teacher. ²¹ And your ears shall hear a word behind you, saying, "This is the way, walk in it," when you turn to the right or when you turn to the left.

— *Isaiah 30:20-21*

Another verse:

¹² Rejoice in hope, be patient in tribulation, be constant in prayer. ¹³ Contribute to the needs of the saints and seek to show hospitality.

— *Romans 12:12-13*

Final verse:

²² Because of the Lord's great love, we are not consumed, for His compassions never fail. ²³ They are new every morning; great is Your faithfulness."

— *Lamentations 3:22-23*

These verses from Isaiah, Paul, and Jeremiah teach us that afflictions and adversity will not last forever. Always remember God's faithfulness and love:

"They are new every morning."

— *Lamentations 3:23*

For Naomi, God allowed her daughter-in-law, Ruth, to stay by her side. As the prophet Isaiah wrote:

"...Your ears will hear a voice behind you saying, 'This is the way; walk in it.'"

— Isaiah 30:21

God will never leave His children helpless.

Now, Naomi and Ruth had settled in Bethlehem. Their daily survival posed the need for some kind of labor or employment to generate income. Ruth said to Naomi:

"Let me see if I can find someone who will help me pick up the grain left in the fields by the harvest workers."

— Ruth 2:1

Naomi replied, "Go ahead, my daughter." Ruth went out to look for work. The harvest season for barley and wheat had just begun. Ruth ended up in a field belonging to Boaz, an affluent merchant in Bethlehem and a relative of her father-in-law, Elimelek.

As the day went by, Ruth was busy picking grain when Boaz arrived at the farm from Bethlehem. It did not take long before Boaz noticed the young woman gleaning among the laborers. Presumably, Ruth must have been an attractive and beautiful lady to command Boaz's quick attention.

The story describes Boaz as a humble man, sensitive to the welfare of his employees. However, Boaz did not pretend not to have noticed Ruth. He asked one of his staff members, "Who is that young woman?"

The staff member replied:

^{6} And the servant who was in charge of the reapers answered, "She is the young Moabite woman who came back with Naomi from the country of Moab. ^{7} She said, 'Please let me glean and gather among the sheaves after the reapers.' So she came, and she has continued from early morning until now, except for a short rest."

— *Ruth 2:6-7*

Ruth was not only favored and promoted but eventually became a benefactor of Boaz's estate. This was the result of her faithfulness, dedication, and character. Note the testimony of her manager after just one day of work:

"She has been working all morning without a moment's rest."

Apostle Paul, in his teaching to the Thessalonians, emphasized the importance of dedication, perseverance, and hard work:

¹¹ and to aspire to live quietly, and to mind your own affairs, and to work with your hands, as we instructed you, ¹² so that you may walk properly before outsiders and be dependent on no one.

— 1 Thessalonians 4:11-12

The testimony of Ruth's dedication and attitude to work mesmerized Boaz. He approached Ruth and said:

⁸ Then Boaz said to Ruth, "Now, listen, my daughter, do not go to glean in another field or leave this one, but keep close to my young women. ⁹ Let your eyes be on the field that they are reaping, and go after them. Have I not charged the young men not to touch you? And when you are thirsty, go to the vessels and drink what the young men have drawn."

— Ruth 2:8-9

What could have happened to Ruth on her first day at the farm without any clue on how to glean grain? *Divine promotion and acceleration.*

Not only had Ruth secured employment, but she had also been granted royal immunity and Hebrew security clearance from Boaz, a man of affluence and authority. Her situation changed due to her step of faith in the God of Israel.

This faith that changed Ruth's life is available to all of us. E.G. White offers a perspective on how to navigate abundant life in *The Ministry of Healing*:

> *"God has formed laws to govern every part of our constitution, and these laws, which He has placed in our being, are divine. For every transgression, there is a fixed penalty, which sooner or later must be realized…*
>
> *"…All our enjoyment or suffering may be traced to obedience or transgression of natural law."*

In essence, White emphasizes that it is humanity's responsibility to follow the basic principles of natural law:

> *"The surrender of hurtful indulgences requires sacrifice. But in the end, it will be found that nature, untrammeled, does her work wisely and well. Those who persevere in obedience to her laws will reap the reward in health of body and health of mind."*

For Ruth, her position at Boaz's farm was a done deal. Overwhelmed with gratitude, she knelt on the ground and asked:

> *"Why have I found such favor in your eyes that you notice me—a foreigner?"*

Boaz replied:

> *[10] Then she fell on her face, bowing to the ground, and said to him, "Why have I found favor in your eyes that you should take notice of me since I am a foreigner?" [11] But Boaz answered her, "All that you have done for your mother-in-law since the death of your husband has been fully told to me, and how you left your father and mother and your native land and came to a people that*

> *you did not know before. [12] The* LORD *repay you for what you have done, and a full reward be given you by the* LORD*, the God of Israel, under whose wings you have come to take refuge!" [13] Then she said, "I have found favor in your eyes, my lord, for you have comforted me and spoken kindly to your servant, though I am not one of your servants."*
>
> *[14] And at mealtime, Boaz said to her, "Come here and eat some bread and dip your morsel in the wine." So she sat beside the reapers, and he passed to her roasted grain. And she ate until she was satisfied, and she had some left over.*
>
> **— *Ruth 2:10-14***

Ruth sat with the harvesters to eat her meal. Boaz offered her some roasted grain, and she ate until she was satisfied and even had leftovers to take home. Boaz instructed his workers:

> *[15] When she rose to glean, Boaz instructed his young men, saying, "Let her glean even among the sheaves and do not reproach her. [16] And also pull out some from the bundles for her and leave it for her to glean, and do not rebuke her."*
>
> **— *Ruth 2:15-16***

Boaz went above and beyond, extending kindness and generosity to Ruth. How many men of wealth and authority would maintain civility and respect toward a foreign woman in need without exploiting her vulnerability?

If you are among the fortunate and privileged, do you exploit the poor and needy for personal gain? If so, Boaz and Ruth have written a lesson on character, compassion, and love.

Remember, it is never too late to repent and start over. Our Heavenly Father is a God of second chances. The story of Ruth and Naomi is a testimony to God's redemptive power.

Ruth could hardly wait to get home to share her breathtaking encounter with Naomi about Boaz, the CEO of Boaz Farms.

As soon as Ruth unpacked her gift and gave some to Naomi, her mother-in-law was astounded. Looking at the packages, Naomi could not wait and burst out with a question:

> *[19] And her mother-in-law said to her, "Where did you glean today? And where have you worked? Blessed be the man who took notice of you." So she told her mother-in-law with whom she had worked and said, "The man's name with whom I worked today is Boaz." [20] And Naomi said to her daughter-in-law, "May he be blessed by the LORD, whose kindness has not forsaken the living or the dead!" Naomi also said to her, "The man is a close relative of ours, one of our redeemers." [21] And Ruth the Moabite said, "Besides, he said to me, 'You shall keep close by my young men until they have finished all my harvest.'" [22] And Naomi said to Ruth, her daughter-in-law, "It is good, my daughter, that you go out with his young women, lest in another field you be assaulted."*

— *Ruth 2:19-22*

The story, as reported by *Bethlehem Times*, suggests that Ruth became acclimated to her work environment and began to socialize with her co-workers. As days went by, Ruth learned not only how to glean barley but also how to glean wheat. Her admiration and affection for Boaz became apparent, and Naomi was not blind to the feelings blossoming between them. Naomi saw in Ruth's emotions a reflection of Solomon's poetic words:

> *"The passion of love bursting into flame is more powerful than death, stronger than the grave. Love cannot be drowned by oceans or floods; it cannot be bought, no matter what is offered."*

> **— *Song of Songs 8:6b-7***

Naomi could no longer bear to watch her beloved daughter-in-law burn with unspoken emotions. So, she devised a plan to bring Ruth and Boaz closer together. She instructed Ruth:

> *"Tonight, he (Boaz) will be winnowing barley on the threshing floor. Wash, put on perfume, and get dressed in your best clothes. Then go down to the threshing floor, but don't let him know you are there until he has finished eating and drinking. When he lies down, note the place where he is lying. Then go and uncover his feet and lie down. He will tell you what to do."*

> **— *Ruth 3:2b-4***

Naomi's advice reflected her wisdom and her deep care for Ruth. She had Ruth's best interests at heart and was determined to help her find a good husband and a great home. Boaz, as a close relative of Elimelek and a man of honor, was an ideal prospect.

Ruth, nervous yet trusting, pondered her mother-in-law's counsel. She treasured the advice but wondered if her actions might come across as desperate. Despite her apprehension, her love and trust for Naomi overshadowed all other concerns. Ruth replied:

"I will do whatever you say."

— Ruth 3:5

She followed Naomi's plan. Ruth waited patiently until Boaz finished his daily routine, ate his dinner, and drank his wine. When he lay down in the grain storage area to sleep, Ruth carefully approached.

Determined to secure her destiny, Ruth uncovered Boaz's feet and lay down as instructed. Startled in the middle of the night, Boaz turned and discovered a woman lying at his feet.

⁹ He said, "Who are you?" And she answered, "I am Ruth, your servant. Spread your wings over your servant, for you are a redeemer." ¹⁰ And he said, "May you be blessed by the LORD, my daughter. You have made this last kindness greater than the first in that you have not gone after young men, whether poor or rich. ¹¹ And now,

> *my daughter, do not fear. I will do for you all that you ask, for all my fellow townsmen know that you are a worthy woman.* ¹² *And now it is true that I am a redeemer. Yet there is a redeemer nearer than I.*

— ***Ruth 3:9-12***

Boaz was a man of integrity who valued Hebrew law and tradition, even above emotional pressure. As he aged, he recognized the need for human affection, love, and companionship, which promote long life, abundant living, and eternal inheritance.

For Ruth, the act of uncovering Boaz's feet demonstrated a natural interest in affection and intimacy. Some scholars interpret this act differently, with some suggesting it was a move to entice Boaz into an inappropriate encounter.

Before judging Ruth's actions, however, it is essential to consider her background. Ruth's culture and traditions as a Moabite differed greatly from Hebrew customs. Moreover, Naomi and her family may not have introduced Ruth to Hebrew religious practices. As a Gentile, Ruth's previous religion might not have condemned her actions, as free women in her culture could openly seek relationships.

Nevertheless, Naomi's advice to Ruth was justified. Ruth was already under the covenant of levirate marriage, and Boaz, being a close relative, was a legitimate prospect. Naomi, as a wise mother-in-law and a loving friend, had Ruth's best interests at heart.

CHAPTER FIVE

THE GOSPEL

The sequential order of the New Testament – Matthew, Mark, Luke, and John. The New Testament books are known as the gospels, which means "good news," based on the new covenant teachings and command of Jesus Christ:

"Go and make disciples"

— *Matthew 28:19-20*

From the day of creation, God never hid the plan of His Son – Jesus – from humanity. God identified Him as a "seed of a woman." As Satan took hold of Adam and Eve through the sin of disobedience in the Garden of Eden, man's failure created a void and separation between him and God. The Lord promised to send a Savior to Earth to destroy the power of Satan and redeem His creation, which He loved:

> *"And I will put enmity between you and the woman, and between your offspring and hers; he will crush your head, and you will strike his heel."*

— *Genesis 3:15*

This passage, Genesis 3:15, is a revelation of God's divine plan to send His Son, who will destroy the power of Satan on Earth and bring salvation to His handiwork (man). Look at the depth of the metaphoric expression:

> *"...he will crush your head."*

This is a hydra-nuclear assault in God's spiritual warfare and the war that broke out between the angels and the dragon:

> *"Now have come the salvation and the power and the kingdom of our God, and the authority of His Messiah.*
>
> *For the accuser of our brothers and sisters, who accuses them before our God day and night, has been hurled down.*
>
> *They triumphed over him by the blood of the Lamb and by the word of their testimony; they did not love their lives so much as to shrink from death."*

— *Revelation 12:10-11*

This victory to overcome Satan and his co-hosts could only be possible through the sacrifice of the Lamb of God for the atonement of our sins. It is only through the Son of God that this victory can be accomplished and sustained.

Paul, in one of his epistles, assures us that we are conquerors and that if God is with us, who can be against us?

"And who is the one that condemns? No one.

Who shall separate us from the love of Christ?

For your sake, we face death all day long; we are considered as sheep to be slaughtered.

For I am convinced that neither death nor life, neither angels nor demons, neither the present nor the future, nor any powers, neither height nor depth, nor anything else in all creation, will be able to separate us from the love of God that is in Christ Jesus our Lord."

— *Romans 8:34-39*

Paul explains that God acquainted Jesus with grief and sorrow. Jesus became our advocate and high priest, filled with God's anointing, as our advocate and intercessor for all our unrighteousness.

So, the issues of Jesus as the Son, the Savior, and the Messiah were already settled in Heaven by the Father – God – before His birth by the Virgin Mary.

Prophet Micah, like many other prophets, had the revelation of where He was going to be born before His birth on Earth:

> *"But you, Bethlehem Ephrathah, though you are small among the clans of Judah, out of you will come for me one who will be ruler over Israel, whose origins are from of old, from ancient times."*

— *Micah 5:2*

There is a legal language in our courts of law that helps substantiate the innocence of accused defenders in the presence of the judge and jury to prove beyond a reasonable doubt. This statement gives the accused the opportunity to present their case in the presence of the court.

A similar scenario can be applied to the case of this study, *"The Audacity of Jesus."* This book you are holding can equally claim that it has proved beyond a reasonable doubt that Jesus Christ of Nazareth is the Son of God, the Messiah, and the Savior, sent by God the Father to redeem mankind, based on the prophetic studies, research, and investigations presented in previous chapters of this book.

Happily, join me and Joseph to welcome Mary from her august visit to Elizabeth. Now, it is very obvious that Mary is pregnant because her physical appearance has changed. The protrusion of her belly is on the horizon; the fact can no longer be hidden from Joseph.

Mary is in this marriage for better or worse. She is determined to succeed and to win with Joseph, her espoused (engaged) husband. Her visit to Elizabeth brought great joy, excitement, and reassurance of God's magnificent blessings and prophetic anointing.

However, deep in her mind, she was broken and fearful about what the outcome of breaking the news of her pregnancy to Joseph would result in, irrespective of all the comforting words of the angel—"Don't be afraid, for you have found favor with God"—and Elizabeth. After all, Mary was very young, vulnerable, and human.

The knowledge of the penalty of death by stoning a woman found to be pregnant out of wedlock in Israel overwhelmed her curiosity and judgment. Her faith waned as she waited for Joseph's reaction and acceptance.

The humble Joseph loved Mary as anyone in a similar situation would love their partner. Love and marriage during adolescence often portray the romantic, passionate affection found in novels like *Romeo and Juliet*.

Joseph, frozen and shocked, might have only been able to utter one phrase, we can imagine: "I AM OUT..." However, the scripture says:

> *"Because Joseph, her husband, was faithful to the law and yet did not want to expose her to public disgrace, he had in mind to divorce her quietly."*

— Matthew 1:19

Joseph's discovery of Mary's pregnancy set his mind and emotions in different directions. Divorcing Mary quietly was an option but not a solution because he was in love with his beautiful Mary. He might have thought:

"This is now bone of my bones and flesh of my flesh..."

However, as Joseph wrestled with his options, he fell asleep. The angel of God appeared to him in a dream and ministered to his spirit.

This angelic visitation is a valuable lesson for many of God's children today. Often, when we are heavy-laden and beseech with problems and afflictions, we run to friends and family for help without waiting on the Lord first. We seek God last, which is wrong and has misled many of God's children.

Joseph had a problem. He had family and friends, but he waited as he considered his options. Always remember God's promise to Joshua and to every one of His children who believe:

"I will never leave you nor forsake you."

—*Joshua 1:5b*

God did not abandon Joseph, and He will not abandon you either. That trouble you think is insurmountable—remember, with God, "All things are possible" to those who believe.

Joseph waited upon the Lord as he considered his options. The angel of the Lord said to him:

> *"Joseph, son of David, do not be afraid to take Mary home as your wife because what is conceived in her is from the Holy Spirit.*
>
> *She will give birth to a son, and you are to give him the name Jesus because he will save his people from their sins."*

— *Matthew 1:20b-21*

Apostle Matthew, in chapter one, verse twenty-three, confirmed the word of the Lord through the prophet, which said:

> *"The virgin will conceive and give birth to a son, and they will call him Immanuel, meaning 'God with us.'"*

Joseph woke from his sleep and obeyed the instructions of the angel. He took Mary home to be his beloved wife. However, Joseph did not consummate the marriage through intimacy until Jesus was born.

In a certain year, King Caesar Augustus ordered a census of all Roman citizens in his empire. Everyone was required to return to their hometown to be counted. Joseph decided to travel to Bethlehem in Judea, a town of David, to be counted. Accompanying him was Mary, his wife, who was close to her delivery date.

While on their way to Bethlehem, Mary went into labor, and Joseph was forced to seek a safe place for her to deliver the baby.

The story goes that Joseph found a traveler's inn. Unfortunately, they were out of luck—the inn was fully booked. However, a kind innkeeper offered them a cave, typically used for keeping animals (such as donkeys that carried loads), for lodging. Mary, likely in labor pain, could not wait any longer.

Colleen Reece reflects on this poignant experience of Mary and Joseph as they struggled to deliver the Deliverer, "Jesus of Nazareth:"

> *"Mary, a gentle hand pressed her shoulder. She returned from her remembrances.*
>
> *'We have reached Bethlehem.'*
>
> *A sharp pain tore through her. 'It is a good thing,' she gasped and laced her fingers together over her swollen belly."*

Many people from the Middle Eastern region of the world, born fifty years ago or earlier, could relate to such experiences. Donkeys were commonly used as a means of transportation and carriage.

The agony dissipated as the cry of a little baby boy broke the silence—Jesus was safely born to the virgin Mary.

Who could imagine the relief, joy, and excitement that filled the hearts of Mary and her husband, Joseph? Immediately, the words of the angel resonated in her heart as promised:

"For with God, all things are possible."

— ***Matthew 1:37***

The baby was named Jesus and Immanuel, as prophesied by the prophet Isaiah and according to the instructions of the angel of the Lord

. Administered by one who is the perfect king, perfect prophet, and perfect priest, it then appeals to men to repent.

G. Campbell Morgan

Jesus' appeal to "Repent, for the kingdom of God is at hand (near)," is the centripetal force of God's "WILL": in His Son, His ministry and mission presented through His messages—the gospel. This was not merely a mystery, nor an evolutionary coincidence, nor a cosmic eruption; rather, it was purely an orchestration of a divine order, a divine mandate primed with a divine manifesto:

"Rather, for the kingdom of God is at hand."

On this ecclesiastical premise, the word of God, who "became a human being (flesh) and lived among us," was set in stone at the beginning of creation. As a result of the failure of Adam and Eve, God made a promise of the Redeemer as He spoke to Satan:

"I will put enmity between thee and the woman, and between thy seed and her seed: it shall bruise thy head, and thou shalt bruise his heel." Genesis 3:15

Yes, what a compassionate and loving God! Who foresaw the future plight of His magnificent creation and handiwork (Genesis 1:21-22, 1:26, 1:31). Adam and Eve were warned not to eat from the forbidden tree, but they did—Satan exploited the vulnerability of the weaker sex. Eve betrayed human loyalty and obedience to the fallen Satan. What chaos and arbitrary submission at the altar of hydno-trialphobia! Human death was the consequence. Yet, the love and mercy of a glorious Father-God allowed the judgment of forbearance: a later eternal death instead of instant death; Adam's son killed his younger brother Abel (Genesis 4:1, 8). Humanity could have remained immortal if they had not eaten from the tree of life. The choice of Adam and Eve to eat from the forbidden tree gave Satan and sin the power to corrupt and rule the world.

"They brag out loud about their stupid nonsense. And by being vulgar and crude, they trap people who have barely escaped from living the wrong kind of life. They promise freedom to everyone. But they are merely slaves of filthy living, because people are slaves of whatever controls them." 2 Peter 2:18-19

Therefore, Jesus, the eternal Word of God, is introduced in the Gospel to educate, appeal to, teach, and disciple believers and Christians in the belief that Jesus is the prophetic Messiah and Savior, the Son of God. The call to repent of sins through confession and baptism, based on faith in Jesus Christ, will lead to eternal life (John 20:31). Matthew, Mark, Luke, and John, the synoptic Gospel writers, symbolically present Jesus as the gift and source of eternal life. This can only be realized by believing in the faith that Jesus is "the way, the truth, and the life"; therefore, everyone who believes in Jesus is made right with God through faith and salvation.

Hence, it is essential to examine the message of the Son of God—Jesus—to establish His Kingdom, Kingship, Sovereignty, divine purpose, sonship (Son of Man), and the full grace of God, and to consider its application to the Church and the world. These elements will define the foundation and mission of Jesus based on the four synoptic Gospels.

The leaders in Jerusalem—the Sanhedrin, Pharisees, Scribes, and priests—rejected the Son of God and His message of the Kingdom. Therefore, they lost the golden opportunity to herald the good news to the temple and the Christian community. The salvation and grace of God could neither fit into the spiritual confines of Judaism nor submit to the audacious manipulations of the poor and the lowly. The Kingdom was at hand, and the time was fulfilled. They could not identify Jesus as the prophesied Messiah, but rather as a prophet of old. They assumed Jesus was the reincarnated Elijah who had returned to mankind.

"To what can I compare this generation? It is like children playing a game in the public square. They complain to their friends: 'We played wedding songs, and you didn't dance, so we played funeral songs, and you didn't mourn.'" Matthew 11:16-17

Jesus' campaign began alone, and His invitation extended to the first four fishermen: Simon (Peter), Andrew, his brother James, and his brother John. As Jesus met these men, His invitation was simple, but His command and charge remained a mystery:

"And Jesus said unto them, 'Come ye after me, and I will make you to become fishers of men.' And straightway they forsook their nets and followed Him." Mark 1:16

The people of Galilee in Judea were lowly, and the religion of Judaism had adversely resonated within their souls and spirits, as they had been compromised by the rulers of the government. The appeal of Jesus' invitation to the fishermen and their reception and acceptance herald and applaud the messianic message and the call to discipleship. Their abandonment of the family business and profession to follow Jesus speaks of "Heaven brought down to earth and to men: hungering and thirsting souls that had waited long for redemption now feasting upon the grace of a merciful Savior."

Jesus boldly declared:

"The time is fulfilled, and the kingdom of God is at hand; repent ye, and believe the gospel."

Thus, this message of "Time" spoken by Jesus himself was a prophetic confirmation of the prophecy of the period, which had already been declared in the Old Testament prophecy made known to the angel Gabriel and God's servant Daniel:

"A period of seventy (weeks) set of seven has been decreed for your people and your holy city to finish their rebellion, to put an end to their sin, to atone for their guilt, to bring in everlasting righteousness, to confirm the prophetic vision, and to anoint the most holy place.

Now listen and understand! Seven sets of seven plus sixty-two sets of seven will pass from the time the command is given to rebuild Jerusalem until a ruler—the Anointed One—comes. Jerusalem will be rebuilt with streets and strong defenses, despite the perilous times." (Daniel 9:24-25)

We should always remember that a day in prophecy represents a year (Num. 14:34 and Eze. 4:6). Therefore, the seventy weeks, or four hundred and ninety days, is equivalent to four hundred and ninety years. The scripture is quite clear on the issue of the set period of beginning time: "The commandment to restore and rebuild Jerusalem unto the Messiah the Prince shall be seven weeks and threescore and two weeks" (Daniel 9:25). This decree by Artaxerxes Longimanus was issued in B.C. 457 (Ezra 6:14 and 7:1). By A.D. 27, Jesus the Messiah was baptized, and the Holy Spirit followed thereafter, marking the beginning of His ministry as prophesied by the prophet Daniel. Jesus confirmed this at the onset of His ministry by proclaiming:

"THE TIME IS FULFILLED."

See Daniel (26-27), which provides the complete prophetic message about Jesus and the birth of His mission and message on earth. The angel Gabriel, who is next to the

Son of God, delivered the message to the prophet Daniel. The same angel was sent by Christ to John to reveal and convey the words of the prophecy that John wrote in the book of Revelation (Rev. 1:3).

John became the last voice in biblical scripture to announce and reveal the fulfillment of Old Testament prophecies:

"God will bless everyone who reads this prophecy to others, and He will bless everyone who hears and obeys it. The time is almost here." Revelation 1:3

God reveals His plans and intentions for mankind to His children through a chosen few—the prophets. Even individuals who are neither trained nor born into the family of the Levites were used by Almighty God to fulfill His prophetic assignments. Amos from the tribe of Judah was among such men. God sent His messages through him, and he became a prophet as he prophesied:

"Surely the LORD God will do nothing, but He revealeth His secret unto His servants the prophets. The lion hath roared, who will not fear? The LORD God hath spoken, who can but prophesy?" Amos 3:7

Jesus began His ministry with a divine manifesto:

"THE KINGDOM OF GOD IS AT HAND."

The hearts of men had been warned and prepared before the entrance of Jesus into ministry through prophetic announcements by the prophets. Yet many people turned a deaf ear to the messages and scriptures concerning the coming of the Messiah. Jesus' ministry on earth aimed to ensure that men understood the message of the kingdom as a foundational aspect of his mission; he employed tapestry and illustrations as he shared captivating stories with his followers. He refused to bore them with strange, dramatic words; instead, he drew from their common local environment and its features, as seen in the lesson about the fig tree, which was familiar to them.

"When you see a fig tree putting out leaves, you know that summer will soon come. So, when you see these things happening, you know that God's kingdom will soon be here. You can be sure that some people of this generation will still be alive when all of this takes place. The sky and the earth won't last forever, but my words will." Luke 21:29-33

The message of the kingdom could also be seen as what I would describe as a "dual-course meal" appeal. While he launched and taught about the new kingdom, Jesus was also preparing the world for his second coming. He charged his followers with warnings against discouragement, distractions, and falling away from the grace of God.

"Don't spend all your time thinking about eating or drinking or worrying about life. If you do, the final day will suddenly catch you like a trap. That day will surprise everyone on earth.

Watch out and keep praying that you escape all that is going to happen and that the Son of Man will be pleased with you." Luke 21:34-36

Jesus' message of the kingdom transcended not only to his disciples but to many others, including one of the major persecutors of the early Christian converts, Saul, who later became an "adjutant general" for Jesus and the economy of the kingdom—Paul.

In one of his epistles to the Thessalonians, as the message of the kingdom resonated with his spirit, Paul, with a conscience of repentance, wrote in his letter as follows:

"But ye, brethren, are not in darkness, that that day should overtake you as a thief. Ye are all the children of light, and the children of the day: we are not of the night, nor of darkness.

Therefore, let us not sleep, as do others, but let us watch and be sober." 1 Thessalonians 5:4-6

Let us examine G. Campbell Morgan's perspective on the kingdom of God. In this analysis, he urges men to "behold the king, understand the kingdom, and meditate in the light of the fact that repentance is the submission of life to the standard of the kingdom and the throne of the king." The understanding here is that the king, the kingdom, and the power of his sovereignty are the crux and foundation of the "good news"—the gospel. Campbell, in furtherance of this argument, submits:

"'At Caesarea Philippi, Jesus said to Peter, "I will give unto thee the keys of the kingdom." He also declared to his disciples, after instructing them in the mysteries of the kingdom, that every scribe instructed in the kingdom of heaven "is like unto a man that is a householder, which bringeth forth out of his treasure things new and old." The world today can only understand the meaning of the kingship and kingdom of God through the church."

The message of the kingdom, in light of the gospel, must obligate not only the followers and Christians but the church to be responsible for the manifestations of the gifts of the kingdom: righteousness and the governance of the Holy Spirit.

"NO PROPHET IS ACCEPTED IN HIS OWN COUNTRY."

"The Spirit of the LORD is upon me, because he hath anointed me to preach the gospel to the poor; he hath sent me to heal the brokenhearted, to preach deliverance to the captives, and recovery of sight to the blind, to set at liberty them that are bruised, to preach the acceptable year of the LORD." Luke 4:16-17

Jesus entered the synagogue on the Sabbath in Galilee to fellowship with the brethren. In the absence of a rabbi, Jesus was chosen to read from the scroll and to lead the service. He began his ministry alone. As he traveled along the shore of Lake Galilee, he met two brothers, Simon and his brother Andrew. Apostle Mark reported that they were fishermen casting their nets into the lake. Jesus approached them and asked them to follow him. In obedience, they followed Jesus. As they continued to walk, they came across the two sons of Zebedee—James and John. They were by the shore, mending their nets inside the boat.

Jesus invited them to join him, and they left their father behind, along with their laborers, to follow the Son of God. All four disciples were with him at the Sabbath meeting. The members present at the meeting were amazed at the authority with which Jesus taught. There was a significant difference in the clarity and wisdom of his teaching in the congregation.

The passage Jesus was reading from the scroll came from the book of Isaiah (Luke 4:16-17).

While the meeting was ongoing, a man with an evil spirit entered the temple and shouted:

"Jesus of Nazareth, what do you want with us? Have you come to destroy us? I know who you are! You are God's holy one." (Mark 1:24)

Jesus commanded the evil spirit, "Be quiet and come out of the man!" The spirit gave a loud shout and left him. The crowd marveled in awe and questioned, "What kind of teacher is this? What new teaching is this—that even the evil spirits obey him?"

The miraculous news spread all over Galilee. A multitude of people began to follow him wherever he went, and many sick individuals were healed. Yet, many people rejected him, and in doubt, they asked:

"Isn't this the carpenter's son?"

Matthew, in his letter, recorded that "Large crowds followed Jesus from Galilee and the region around the ten cities known as Decapolis" (Matt. 4:25). Jesus continued to gather men for stewardship; they left their families to follow him. Over time, a number of young, devoted men increased and became known as the disciples. Jesus taught and empowered them spiritually by exemplifying the meaning of the kingdom of God through local illustrations and parables. Many crowds followed them.

JESUS HEALS MANY SICK PEOPLE

"Jesus traveled throughout the region of Galilee, teaching in the synagogues and announcing the good news about the kingdom. He healed every kind of disease and illness. News about him spread as far as Syria, and people soon began bringing to him all who were sick. Whatever their sickness or disease, or if they were demon-possessed, epileptic, or paralyzed—he healed them all" (Matthew 4:23-24).

Jesus' ministry in Galilee became the foundation of his gospel message: "Repent, for the kingdom of God is at hand." His compassion to heal the sick was a game-changer in the history of Judaism and Christianity in the land of Palestine and Israel.